Lament for a Nation

photo: William Christian

Lament for a Nation

The Defeat of Canadian Nationalism

George Grant

The Carleton Library Series No. 50

CARLETON UNIVERSITY PRESS

THE CARLETON LIBRARY SERIES

A series of original works, new collections, and reprints of source material relating to
Canada, issued under the supervision of the Editorial Board, Carleton Library Series,
Carleton University Press Inc., Ottawa, Canada.

ISBN 0-88629-257-3 (paperback)

Printed and bound in Canada.
Distributed by Oxford University Press Canada,
70 Wynford Drive, Don Mills, Ontario, Canada, M3C 1J9, (416) 441-2941

Carleton University Press gratefully acknowledges the support extended to its publishing
programme by the Canada Council and the financial assistance of the Ontario Arts
Council. The Press would also like to thank the Department of Canadian Heritage,
Government of Canada and the Government of Ontario through the Ministry of Culture,
Tourism and Recreation for their assistance.

CANADIAN CATALOGUING IN PUBLICATION DATA
Grant George, 1918–1988
   Lament for a nation : the defeat of Canadian nationalism

(Carleton library series ; 50)
New ed.
Previously published 1970 as no. 50 in the Carleton library series.
ISBN 0-88629-257-3

1. Nationalism – Canada.   2. Canada – Politics and government.
3. Canada – Relations – United States.   4. United States – Relations – Canada.
I. Title.   II. Series.

FC98.G73 1994   971.064   C95-900035-6
F1034.2.G74 1994

JUL   9 1997

Contents

To Derek Bedson and Judith Robinson

TWO LOVERS OF THEIR COUNTRY

ONE LIVING AND ONE DEAD

Introduction to the Carleton Library Edition

THE CARLETON LIBRARY HAS KINDLY suggested the reissuing of this book – 'kindly' because it is a book written out of particular events, and one therefore in which any general truths arise in the context of circumstances eight years old. It is a disadvantage these days for any general thesis to be tied to past events, because eight years seems more than a generation. Our memories are killed in the flickering images of the media, and the seeming intensity of events. There is weakened in us the simplest form of that activity of re-collection which Plato knew to be the chief means to wisdom.

It may be well therefore to preface a new edition by asking the question: how do we stand in 1970 compared with 1963? The central problem for nationalism in English-speaking Canada has always been: in what ways and for what reasons do we have the power and the desire to maintain some independence of the American empire? (It would be impertinent indeed to define what is the chief problem for French-speaking nationalism.) On the surface it is certainly much easier in 1970 than it was in 1963 for Canadians not to want to be swallowed by the U.S. The years of the Vietnam war have been an exposition (a veritable Expo) of the American empire. It does not take much intelligence or patriotism to be glad that one's children are not drafted for that war. The mainland of that empire no longer seems so rewarding a place to live. Even the Canadian bourgeoisie can see the perhaps unresolvable racial conflict, the expansion and decay of its cities, the increase of military influence in constitutional life, the breakdown between the generations, the effects of a century of environmental spoliation, etc. etc. In 1963 we could swim or go fishing in Lake Erie without cleaning off the excrement. Today nobody can forget Cleveland. Such events make possible a nationalist appeal to many Canadian voters. And underlying the particular difficulties of the empire is the deeper anxiety as to the very possibility of the good life in civilization ruled by the spirit of dynamic technique. This spectre is naturally enough glimpsed most often in the U.S.A. Eight years ago such anxiety was considered nutty reaction; today it stalks the public world.

During the missile crisis of 1963, the U.S.A. was symbolised for us by the Kennedys, who presented American imperialism in the liberal phrasing and middlebrow culture of Camelot. This attracted the Canadian bourgeoisie, who liked to believe that the society which so benefited them was also producing human excellence. How much closer were "Jack and Jackie" to the culture of Forest Hill and Westmount than was the remembering rhetorician from Prince Albert. It was natural for the *Globe and Mail* to be dazzled by the Kennedys. The villains of my book have gone down before the crime of political assassination. Their instrument in Ottawa, Mr. Pearson, has disappeared into whatever limbo awaits the ambitions of self-righteousness. In the U.S. the dominant classes now find themselves in a situation which requires a tighter politics. They must content themselves with the clearer, if grimmer, technocratic skill of Mr. Nixon, and even with the direct bourgeois self-defence of Mr. Agnew and Mr. Mitchell. We are quite proud of our "show-biz" technocrat in Ottawa, when the U.S. can no longer afford that luxury.

In such a situation Canadians are less impelled to rush headlong towards continental integration. On the surface there are many stirrings of nationalism. Indeed, nationalism has a clearer place, even in the present Liberal administration, that it ever had in the King, St. Laurent or Pearson eras of that party. Mr. Trudeau's policies may be inadequate, vacillating, and tailored to please the dominant powers, yet they still show traces of care about Canada which could not have been present in Howe's worship of the corporation, or in the capitalist "internationalism" of Mr. Pearson. Although Mr. Trudeau seems willing to go along with the central Liberal tradition of never offending the large corporations on substantial issues, he seems to make small concessions to our supposed independence. Most hopeful is that among the young, (sometimes in formal politics but more often outside it), the desire for independence is greater than for many generations. Unlike the generation of 1945, which scrambled into the corporations, they have a realistic suspicion of corporation capitalism, and this is after all the negative *sine qua non* of any nationalism.

Nevertheless, below the surface the movement towards integration continues. The immediate reason for this is our position in the empire. We are not in that empire as are the exploited colonies of South America, but rather with the intimacy of a younger brother status. We have all the advantages of that empire, the wealth which pours in from all over the world, the technology which comes to us through the multinational corporations. Yet, because we have formal political independence, we can keep out of some of the dirty work necessary to that empire. We make money from Vietnam; but we do not have to send our sons there. We are like the child of some stockbroker who can enjoy the fruits of his father's endeavours by living the swinging life, but likes to exclude from his mind where the money comes from. Like most other human beings, Canadians want it both ways. We want through formal nationalism to escape the disadvantages of the American dream; yet we also want the benefits of junior membership in the empire. Unfortunately it is the dominant classes in our society who gain particularly from that membership. This general position has been put most absurdly by the Liberal leader in Quebec, M. Bourassa: "American technology, French culture" – as if technology were something external (e.g. machines) and not itself a spirit which excludes all that is alien to itself. As Heidegger has said, technique is the metaphysic of the age.

Lying behind the immediate decisions arising from our status within the empire is the deeper question of the fate of any particularity in the technological age. What happens to nationalist strivings when the societies in question are given over, at the very level of faith, to the realisation of the technological dream? At the core of that faith is service to the process of universalization and homogenization. "The one best

means" must after all be the same in Chicago, Hamilton, and
Dusseldorf. How much difference can there be between societies whose
faith in "the one best means" transcends even communist and capitalist differences? The distinction will surely be minimal between two
nations which share a continent and a language, especially when the
smaller of the two has welcomed with open arms the chief instruments
of its stronger brother – the corporations.

Although our present political status gives us certain advantages
over the U.S., it entails certain disadvantages. Life as little brother often
leads to political naivety and even self-righteousness. We have not
produced such a firmly defined opposition as have the United States.
Not so many of us have been forced to look unflinchingly into the face
of Moloch. In stressing this disadvantage, I do not imply the terrible
Marxist doctrine that we can encourage great political evils because
they are a necessity to later political good. The evil of this doctrine was
exposed when the communists espoused, in its name, political polar-
ization during the Weimar Republic.

This book was written too much from anger and too little from
irony. The ambiguity of the English-speaking Canadian tradition was
therefore not made evident. Our hope lay in the belief that on the
northern half of this continent we could build a community which had
a stronger sense of the common good and of public order than was
possible under the individualism of the American capitalist dream. The
original sources of that hope in the English-speaking part of our society lay in certain British traditions which had been denied in the
American revolution. But the American liberalism which we had to
oppose, itself came out of the British tradition – the liberalism of Locke
and Adam Smith, – which was also to become dominant in England as
well as in the U.S., and which reached its apotheosis and decadence
there in the thought of Keynes and Moore and Forster. The sense of the
common good standing against capitalist individualism depended in
English-speaking Canada on a tradition of British conservatism which
was itself largely beaten in Great Britain by the time it was inherited
by Canadians. Our pioneering conditions also made individualist

capitalist greed the overwhelming force among our élite. But such a spirit could not but express itself as continentalist from the time of the Annexation Manifesto to the present. Many Canadians – in church and state and education – worked against this spirit, and hoped to incarnate certain older traditions from western Europe. But one of the reasons their dreams were vain was that they tried to hold onto these things through Britishness, just at a time when western Europe was turning away from its pre-progressive past and surrendering to the same technological Moloch of war and peace which was to reach its height in the U.S. To put the matter crudely: the irony is seen when one contemplates the fact that in our century the British have abased themselves before American capitalism for the sake of beating the Germans, only to find after two supposed victories that the Germans are more important to their masters than they are themselves. The twentieth century was not a period in which it was wise to rely on British traditions as counter-attractions to the American dream. Yet these were what we had.

I emphasize this failure in irony because many simple people (particularly journalists and professors) took it to be a lament for the passing of a British dream of Canada. It was rather a lament for the romanticism of the original dream. Only a fool could have lived in Toronto in the 1920s and 1930s without recognizing that any British tradition of the common good which transcended contract was only a veneer. Today, the British tradition means that Mr. E.P. Taylor, who has given his life to integrating this country into the capitalist empire, still in the 1970s finds it impossible to pronounce the works "Kentucky Derby" in the proper American fashion.

A serious criticism of the book has been that to write in terms of inevitability (call it if you will fate) is to encourage the flaccid will which excuses the sin of despair in the name of necessity. By writing of the defeat of Canadian nationalism, one encourages in a small way the fulfilment of the prophecy. Most men, when in a weak position, need immanent hopes to keep alive their will to fight against odds. This has obviously been one of the great strengths of Marxists. Their belief that history was on their side has given them the strength to live with courage in times of difficulty and defeat. The accusation would be that I had no business to write of the defeat of Canadian nationalism because in so doing I may have encouraged it.

To answer such a criticism would require a careful discussion of the idea of the noble delusion – that is, the doctrine that the health of any society depends on those who have practical authority being attached to virtue, and that this attachment can often only be sustained by opinions which are less than perfectly true. Whatever might be said of that doctrine, it clearly must be applied in writing with prudence – in the light of the circumstances at hand. We live in an era when most of our public men are held by ignoble delusions – generally a mixture of technological progressivism and personal self-assertion – all that is left of official liberalism in the English-speaking world. In such circumstances a writer has a greater responsibility to ridicule the widespread ignoble delusions than to protect the few remaining beliefs which might result in nobility. In an age when the alternatives often seem to be between planetary destruction and planetary tyranny (and when these alternatives are obvious products of the ignoble delusions of "the age of reason"), protecting romantic hopes of Canadian nationalism is a secondary responsibility.

This criticism is related to a more important one. My writings have often been called pessimistic. The words "optimistic" and "pessimistic" came into the tradition around the thought of Leibniz, and Voltaire's rather shallow criticism of him. They were words describing men's interpretation of the whole. I think the words should be reserved for this purpose and not used loosely about other people's feeling states or particular predictions. It would be the height of pessimism to believe that our society could go on in its present directions without bringing down upon itself catastrophes. To believe the foregoing would be pessimism, for it would imply that the nature of things does not bring forth human excellence.

G.P. Grant
Dundas, 1970.

Foreword

IN HIS 1970 INTRODUCTION to *Lament for a Nation*, Professor George Grant modestly expressed doubt whether his study had an enduring importance beyond the particular circumstances occasioning its appearance. He questioned whether his appeal to the distinctiveness of our political heritage would strike a responsive chord in a generation witnessing other historical events and participating in new social experiences. Yet, Grant's modesty aside, one should urge readers to renew their acquaintance with his passionate defense of our Canadian identity, if for no other reason than that we are still, and perhaps to an even greater extent, subject to widespread homogenizing, continentalist forces which have been shaping our destiny for the past two decades. For those whose lives have been deeply affected by massive continental economic restructuring, who have begun to experience the political and social implications of living within the new continental trade region formed under the North American Free Trade Agreement, and who are attempting to navigate between equally powerful globalizing forces and the recrudescence of fragmenting local attachments, Grant's tocsin still warns with unsurpassed clarity of the dangerous shoals surrounding us.

Grant's essay is of enduring importance, however, beyond the similarities between our own time and the historical circumstances within which *Lament for a Nation* was written. With this study, Professor Grant opened Canadian public debate, with frankness and depth, to include the most fundamental and perennial questions a nation must ask itself about the full meaning of its own political existence. He challenged us to reflect on the unique possibilities and limits constituting our destiny as Canadians. If it took as its point of departure Diefenbaker's opposition to nuclear warheads for the Bomarc missiles and his subsequent resistance to Kennedy's continental defense initiative, Grant's study moved rapidly to broader questions concerning the difficult fate of a people in the modern age, whose experiences and ways of life evidence a complexity and depth greater than the equally pressing force of technological progress. How do forms of human existence in which people traditionally found meaning for their lives, Grant asked, stand in relation to the modern project on behalf of universal liberation and mastery of nature? Was it our fate as modern beings to live out the aridity and flatness of the culture defining the technological empire south of us? Were there phenomena in our own heritage, he challenged, which could sustain some resistance and provide moral ballast to the apparent soulless world order forming around us? Professor Grant confronted, in these questions, the complex issue of how to preserve some compass points amidst forces denying their relevance.

Lament for a Nation should be respected as a masterpiece of political meditation. A meditation raises the reader from what is familiar and near, to a level in which the recollection of experiences and understandings reveals what is most enduring in our human existence. It demands that we reflect on the tension between our particular historical existence and the greater whole of which we are a part. A meditation closes by returning its participants to the familiar and near, having disclosed how they are necessarily invested with what is highest and most enduring.

A political meditation can only be written and understood by those who enjoy friendship with the régime they inhabit. Such civic friendships are not only expressed as contentment with the peace and security afforded by the régime. As Grant admits, Lament for a Nation is written both in anger and in sadness. But, it is also written out of friendship. Anger is in this case the manifestation of righteous indignation, occasioned by a sense of injustice, and born from loyalty to and trust in a tradition of practices to which one believes one owes an allegiance. It draws its life from friendship to a tradition which preserves a "precious good" worthy of great sacrifices. Sadness is the appropriate response to the temporal vicissitudes all friendships must undergo, a melancholic witnessing to the changes and reassessments to which all life is subject. Grant's expressions of anger and sadness simply capture the percolations of friendship, and for this reason should not be seen as arising from resentment or loss of spirit. His is a sort of chastening rhetoric, permitted only by friends; friends whose melancholy works like a homeopathic draught of wormwood.

Lament for a Nation, like Professor Grant's other works, is grounded on the principle that our interpretation of ourselves and what we perceive as meaningful is, in great part, brought forward within a "destiny" or "fate" (a "primal" as he would call it) which precedes our individual efforts and enables us to be the sort of beings we are. He believed that a legacy of accomplishments and meaningful symbols could be a heritage for the present. The "pre-judgements" and "forethoughts" of the primal we inhabit provide the substance of our debates and our actions; they compose the "web" in which all our intercourse occurs. But Grant did not believe that we were ineluctably immured in this historical horizon. We could respond to our "primal," perhaps by resenting its drawing power, or by trying to master it and subject its contents to different values. Ours could also be a response of openness, a reverent respect for the distinctive political and moral possibilities inherent within it. The wager for Canadians was how we would respond to our "primal."

This response would be complex. It is our difficult destiny as Canadians in North America, Professor Grant pointed out, to be faced with contradicting "primals." First, we were part of a tradition whose founding myths, political symbols, and autochthonous experiences constitute our sense of place and belongingness to a land and its culture. Our own is not simply space and time, it is a territory and a history. It is a home crafted by tory strains of respect for the community or nation and recognition of the appropriate cultural practices needed to sustain orderly, political right; by Catholic and Anglican strains of loving stewardship to the divine and a sense of "owingness" to what is beyond human will; and by diverse British philanthropic strains of charity and equality of condition. This had to be contrasted with an empire to the south whose politics affirmed the primacy of individuals and the value of technical skills; whose religion looked, via Reformed Calvinism, to the sovereignty and creativity of the divine will in history as the paradigm for human initiative; and whose economics sanctioned virtually unhindered self-interested enterprise. Our country, Grant would say, was to be different from the United States: it would be a society which was more ordered, more reasonable, more caring, less violent, and less enthused by reckless dreams.

Existing in tension with this heritage, however, was another destiny, equally composing our way in the world. What we are, Grant explained, is also constituted by a milieu whose logic and direction had been unfolding since the beginning of modernity, with the American empire as its most expressive manifestation: being as technology. Grant, indebted here to Heidegger, was later to call the technological spirit of modernity a "complete ontological package," meaning that our institutions, our programs, our laws, our behaviours, our amusements and our self-understandings were all fundamentally echoing its logic. A philosophy of reason as domination over nature, a politics of imperial, bureaucratic administration, a public discourse of efficiency, and a sociology of adjustment and equilibrium were forging, as so many specialized arts of modern technology, a new way for us. Grant's shorthand version of how technology was reshaping us was to speak of its "universalizing" and "homogenizing" effect. Contained within these terms were complex reflections on the modern dream of universal liberation and the prospect of universal tyranny, and on the moral hopes associated with equality and the reality of creeping sameness. Taken together, he was to demonstrate, technology involved a fundamental reshaping of the human spirit and the gradual eclipse or transformation of human experiences that in the past had provided us with moral and intellectual ballast.

An assessment of this second destiny was not as easy as one might expect. It would be otiose, Grant never tired of reminding, to overlook the moral promise and concrete achievements of modern technology. It had made possible, in a way never believed possible, the actualization of the duty of charity and the extension of individual freedom. While it did not carry forth the full spirituality of Christianity's vision of a universal free and equal community, the régime of modern technology had erased the oppressive hierarchies and insular parochialisms impeding the actualization of that vision. While no one should deny this was progress, the question remained, At what cost?

As Grant argues here, and more thematically in his later books, technological progress could not be separated from an accompanying transformation of the human spirit; a transformation which made it impossible to unite the new social controls with traditional moralities and politics. Universalizing and homogenizing, technology's driving principle of "efficiency" demanded the suppression of local differences, particular loyalties, and credible resistances. Whatever lingering pockets of "autochthony" might declare opposition, the spirit of the régime – sustained by its continental ruling class of technicians and administrators, and the officially sanctioned discourse of instrumentality and efficiency – regarded their opposition as nothing more than folly or sentimentality. The new régime, whatever value the fruits of its technical arts and sciences, was a universal tyranny, disagreeably out of tune with the principle that had once sustained the Western world and particularly its North American experiment, namely cultural pluralism and freedom of the spirit.

The fate of Canada was a microcosm of the confrontation of all peoples with the powerfully transforming forces of the West. The expectation that Canadians might recall what within their "primal" constituted a "precious good" worth preserving, or what might be testimony to a spiritually more profound way of being human, had been annulled in the realization that any distinctiveness in Canada's way of life, its skills, and practices, could only appear now as stylized, abstract images circulating through the homogenizing processes of technological efficiency. The same would be true around the globe. The conservative and communitarian strands in our heritage, once understood as containing enduring concepts of what is good for humanity, could now only be seen as mere political ideology or a set of values.

Against this, no simple appeal to the spirit or rootedness of our past sense of belonging to the land could be relevant. To think of containing and embalming the distinctive virtues of that time would be to condemn oneself to antiquarianism or romanticism, if not worse. There could be no return to a past, nor should the spirit of modernity be dampened by willing away what had come to be. Grant, following Nietzsche, had continuously warned of the poisonous "resentment" that lay at the heart of wishing away time's "it was" – a poison that could deprive life of vitality and confidence.

Lament for a Nation is, however, more than a lament of a passing good and a dissection of the non-viability of nationalist or conservative discourse. If it demonstrates the public irrelevance of those discourses, it does not assume their theoretical emptiness. Indeed, the meditation has the effect, with its powerful symbols and chastening rhetoric, to evoke a bittersweet remembrance of our foundations, of the expectations we have of our heroes, and of different stories we tell of our battles and accords. Such remembrance, at the very least, tugs at vestiges of the primal which continues to inspire our self-interpretation. How else could the passionate appeals of Western, Québec, and Maritime nationalists evoke such enthusiasm; how else could our continuing efforts to negotiate and renegotiate satisfactory economic and military ties to our continental neighbours give rise to such debate and emotion; why else would regional separatist agitation inspire such a groundswell of support to renew our political institutions?

The questions Professor Grant demanded we confront still lie at the centre of our current political debates. How can Canada preserve fragments of a way of life and of understandings whose public relevance is doubtful to our ruling élites? Is it necessary to capitulate to the agenda of continentalist expansion, and what are the costs of such multinational efficiency to the Canadian workforce, its culture, social programs, and political independence? Is the promise of a global village, liberated to the latest technological contrivances, the reality of a universal tyranny? And beyond this, have the forces of progress unleashed further forces which are extinguishing not only the confidence in progress but also the commitment to the purposes we believe to be furthered by that progress? Finally, can a régime which has eclipsed the public relevance of experiences of either tradition or transcendence, be humanly satisfying?

Grant posed questions in *Lament for a Nation* which are at the heart of Canada's existence as a nation. He himself offered no simple answers but illuminated the inevitable complexity and ambiguity of such questions as the proper intellectual territory of inquiry for the thinking mind. He was optimistic. We have been able to safeguard the complexity and ambiguity of those answers, and hence our humanity, by moral and political practices which respect plurality, dignity, and our higher purposes, and which abjure quick solutions, absolute certainties, and radical transformations. Grant asked us to ensure the same type of moderation for the present and the future.

A chastening rhetoric both cleanses and purifies. If we were to speak of the enduring significance of *Lament for a Nation*, it would be that Professor Grant challenges us to respond to the deepest demands of our modern existence, both as dwellers on a continent defined by a great imperial power and as participants in the complex project of modernity. He tries to teach us, against all odds, how we can still see what is beautiful and good in our own. Grant asks us to be aware of traces of practices, understandings, ways of life, and lived-experience which are pre-technological in our cultural and political legacy and manifest in "the evident experience of living." He knew we had also to accept the difficult tensions of technological society. His advice is a prescription of steering between local parochialism on the one hand and the deracinated life of the modern universal and homogeneous state on the other. It is a prescription demanding attentiveness and courage.

In the wake of the consensuses and discords of the Meech Lake Agreement and the Charlottetown Accord, the recurring threat of regional separatism, not to say fragmentation along innumerable social cleavages; the controversies and opportunities opened by the new continental trade partnership; and the fractious state of affairs at the international level where Canada continually reassesses its proper role, the courage and moderation counselled by Professor Grant seem as appropriate today as they were in 1963. It is just as important to remind today's political leaders how vital it is to place these new departures in the most comprehensive context – historical and philosophical. This is especially important if we are one day to be called before the bar of history to justify and explain our watershed decisions. Our age seems forever animated by a sort of new-world visionary politics on which such policies seem to ride forward, and by awesome technological power at our behest which can quell all resistances. This makes ours the time requiring the most sustained, responsible, and profound public debates concerning our continued existence. For such debates, *Lament for a Nation* has identified a set of symbols and a cosmion of meaning which might guide us with common sense and integrity, still under-standable as the great guarantors of public decency.

Peter C. Emberley
Carleton University
1994

Chapter One

NEVER HAS SUCH A TORRENT of abuse been poured on any Canadian figure as that during the years from 1960 to 1965. Never have the wealthy and the clever been so united as they were in their joint attack on Mr. John Diefenbaker. It has made life pleasant for the literate classes to know that they were on the winning side. Emancipated journalists were encouraged to express their dislike of the small-town Protestant politician, and they knew they would be well paid by the powerful for their efforts. Suburban matrons and professors knew that there was an open season on Diefenbaker, and that jokes against him at cocktail parties would guarantee the medal of sophistication. New agreements were produced. Such a progressive intellectual as F. H. Underhill ridiculed Diefenbaker in the same accents as the editorials of the *Globe and Mail*. Socialist members of parliament united with the representatives of Toronto and Montreal business to vote his government from office. In my parish in southern Ontario, on the Sunday before the election of 1963, the Holy Eucharist was offered for "stable government," well expressing the unanimity of bourgeois intention. Only the rural and small-town people voted for Diefenbaker *en masse,* but such people are members of neither the ruling nor the opinion-forming classes.

The tide of abuse abated after the election of 1963. The establishment thought that it had broken Diefenbaker and could now afford to patronize him. But Diefenbaker has refused to play dead. He has shown himself capable of something the wealthy and the clever rarely understand – the virtue of courage. The patronizing airs are turning once more into abuse; the editorials and the "news" become increasingly vindictive.

It is interesting to speculate why Diefenbaker raised the concentrated wrath of the established classes. Most of his critics claim that he is dominated by ambition, almost to the point of egomania. They also claimed (while he was still in office) that he was dangerous because he was an astute politician who put personal power first. Yet his actions turned the ruling class into a pack howling for his blood. Astute politicians, who are only interested in political power, simply do not act this way. There must be something false or something missing in this description of his actions. To search for a consistent description is partly why I have written this book.

The search must be related to the title of this meditation. To lament is to cry out at the death or at the dying of something loved. This lament mourns the end of Canada as a sovereign state. Political laments are not usual in the age of progress, because most people think that society always moves forward to better things. Lamentation is not an indulgence in despair or cynicism. In a lament for a child's death, there is not only pain and regret, but also celebration of passed good.

> *I cannot but remember such things were*
> *That were most precious to me.*

In Mozart's great threnody, the Countess sings of *la memoria di quel bene.* One cannot argue the meaninglessness of the world from the facts of evil, because what could evil deprive us of, if we had not some prior knowledge of good? The situation of absolute despair does not allow a man to write. In the theatre of the absurd, dramatists like Ionesco and Beckett do not escape this dilemma. They pretend to absolute despair and yet pour out novels and plays. When a man truly despairs, he does not write; he commits suicide. At the other extreme, there are the saints who know that the destruction of good serves the supernatural end; therefore they cannot lament. Those who write laments may have heard the propositions of the saints, but they do not know that they are true. A lament arises from a condition that is common to the majority of men, for we are situated between despair and absolute certainty.

I have implied that the existence of a sovereign Canada served the good. But can the disappearance of an unimportant nation be worthy of serious grief? For some older Canadians it can. Our country is the only polticial entity to which we have been trained to pay allegiance. Growing up in Ontario, the generation of the 1920's took it for granted that they belonged to a nation. The character of the country was self-evident. To say it was British was not to deny it was North American. To be a Canadian was to be a unique species of North American. Such alternatives as F. H. Underhill's – "Stop being British if you want to be a nationalist" – seemed obviously ridiculous. We were grounded in the wisdom of Sir John A. Macdonald, who saw plainly more than a hundred years ago that the only threat to nationalism was from the South, not from across the sea. To be a Canadian was to build, along with the French, a more ordered and stable society than the liberal experiment in the United States. Now that this hope has been extinguished, we are too old to be retrained by a new master. We find ourselves like fish left on the shores of a drying lake. The element necessary to our existence has passed away. As some form of political loyalty is part of the good life, and as we are not flexible enough to kneel to the rising sun, we must be allowed to lament the passing of what had claimed our allegiance. Even on a continent too dynamic to have memory, it may still be salutary to celebrate memory. The history of the race is strewn with gasping political fish. What makes the gasping comic, in the present case, is its involvement with such ambiguous and contrasting figures as Pearson and Diefenbaker.

Lamenting for Canada is inevitably associated with the tragedy of Diefenbaker. His inability to govern is linked with the inability of this country to be sovereign. In the last years, many writers have described the confusions, contradictions, and failures of the Diefenbaker government. Even when Peter Newman has exuded malice, or Blair Fraser has hidden Liberal propaganda behind the mask of impartiality, their descriptions have often been accurate. Yet their accuracy is made suspect by their total argument. They rejoice that we have back in office the party of the ruling class. They generously allow that the Liberal party had become arrogant by 1957, and that in a "democratic" system it is good to have alternative administrations. (For example, it gives our natural rulers a proper chastening.) But they never grant that, for twenty years before its defeat in 1957, the Liberal party had been pursuing policies that led inexorably to the disappearance of Canada. Its policies led to the impossibility of an alternative to the American republic being built on the northern half of this continent. They never grant that the seeds of Canada's surrender lay in Mackenzie King's régime. This fact and Diefenbaker's inchoate knowledge of it are ignored by the journalists of the establishment. They never allow that when the Conservatives came to office they were faced with a situation that would lead, if not corrected, to the disappearance of their country's independence. No credit is given to the desperate attempts of Diefenbaker and his colleagues to find alternative policies, both national and international, to those of their predecessors.

Diefenbaker's confusions and inconsistencies are, then, to be seen as essential to the Canadian fate. His administration was not an aberration from which Canada will recover under the sensible rule of the established classes. It was a bewildered attempt to find policies that were adequate to its noble cause. The 1957 election was the Canadian people's last gasp of nationalism. Diefenbaker's government was the strident swansong of that hope. Although the Canadian nationalist may be saddened by the failures of Diefenbaker, he is sickened by the shouts of sophisticated derision at his defeat. Those who crowed at Diefenbaker's fall did not understand the policies of government that were essential if Canada was to survive. In their derision they showed, whether they were aware of it or not, that they really paid allegiance to the homogenized culture of the American Empire.

This meditation is limited to lamenting. It makes no practical proposals for our survival as a nation. It argues that Canada's disappearance was a matter of necessity. But how can one lament necessity – or, if you will, fate? The noblest of men love it; the ordinary accept it; the narcissists rail against it. But I lament it as a celebration of memory; in this case, the memory of that tenuous hope that was the principle of my ancestors. The insignificance of that hope in the endless ebb and flow of nature does not prevent us from mourning. At least we can say with Richard Hooker: "Posterity may know we have not loosely through silence permitted things to pass away as in a dream."

Chapter Two

HOW DID DIEFENBAKER CONCEIVE CANADA? Why did the men who
run the country come to dislike and then fear his conception? The
answers demonstrate much about Canada and its collapse.

Most journalists account for Diefenbaker's failure by the foibles of
his personality. Influenced by *Time* magazine, politics is served up as
gossip, and the more titillating the better. The jaded public wants to be
amused; journalists have to eat well. Reducing issues to personalities is
useful to the ruling class. The "news" now functions to legitimize
power, not to convey information. The politics of personalities helps
the legitimizers to divert attention from issues that might upset the
status quo. Huntley and Brinkley are basic to the American way of life.
Canadian journalists worked this way in the election of 1963. Their
purposes were better served by writing of Diefenbaker's "indecision,"
of Diefenbaker's "arrogance," of Diefenbaker's "ambition," than by
writing about American-Canadian relations. Indeed, his personality
was good copy. The tragedy of his leap to unquestioned power, the
messianic stance applied to administrative detail, the prairie rhetoric
murdering the television – these are an essential part of the
Diefenbaker years. But behind all the stories of arrogance and indecision, there are conflicts – conflicts over principles. The man had a
conception of Canada that threatened the dominant classes. This
encounter is the central clue to the Diefenbaker administration. The
political actions of men are ultimately more serious than the gossip of
Time and *Newsweek* will allow.

All ruling classes are produced by the societies they are required to
rule. In the 1960's, state capitalism organizes a technological North
America. The ruling classes are those that control the private govern-

ments (that is, the corporations) and those that control the public government which co-ordinates the activities of these corporations. North America is the base of the world's most powerful empire to date, and this empire is in competition with other empires. The civilians and soldiers who run its military operations increasingly crowd its corridors of power.[1]

Since 1960, Canada has developed into a northern extension of the continental economy. This was involved in the decisions made by C. D. Howe and his men. Our traditional role – as an exporter of raw materials (particularly to Europe) with highly protected industry in central Canada – gradually lost its importance in relation to our role as a branch-plant of American capitalism. Our ruling class is composed of the same groups as that of the United States, with the signal difference that the Canadian ruling class looks across the border for its final authority in both politics and culture. As Canada is only gradually being called upon to play a full role in United States' world policies, our military is less influential at home than is the case in the United States. Of all the aspects of our society, the military is the most directly an errand boy for the Americans.

Our rulers, particularly whose who enjoy wielding power, move in and out of the corporations, the civil service, and politics. For example, Mitchell Sharp was a leading civil servant under C.D. Howe, directing the development of our resources by continental capitalism. With the fall of the Liberals, he had to move to Brazilian Traction. He had the gumption, however, to be interested in the revival of the Liberal party at its lowest ebb, and so today he exercises power as Minister of Trade

1   The use of the concept "American Empire" is often objected to, particularly by those who like to believe that the age of empires is over. They associate an empire with earlier patterns – the British, the Spanish, and the French – when Europeans maintained rule in distant parts of the globe by superior arms and control of the sea. But an empire does not have to wield direct political control over colonial countries. Poland and Czechoslovakia are as much part of the Russian Empire as India was of the British, or Canada and Brazil of the American. An empire is the control of one state by another. In this sense, the United States of America has an empire.

and Commerce. The political members of the ruling class live more precariously than the businessmen and the civil servants, but if successful they have the pleasures of public power. For instance, it did not appear likely, before the election of 1957, that Pearson would be the leader of the Liberal party. A civil servant who had turned Minister of External Affairs was not close to the heart of those creating the new Canada from 1945 to 1957. Yet after the election of 1957, when many Liberal leaders immediately retreated into the cover of the corporations, he had the courage to stay with the inconveniences of politics. Today he and his friends have direct control over the government. On the other hand, Robert Winters, who could not stomach the inconveniences of opposition, must content himself with running Rio Tinto and York University.

From 1940 to 1957, the ruling class of this country was radically reshaped. In 1939, the United Kingdom still seemed a powerful force, and the men who ruled Canada were a part of the old Atlantic triangle. They turned almost as much to Great Britain as to the United States, economically, culturally, and politically. After 1940, the ruling class found its centre of gravity in the United States. During the long years of Liberal rule, the strength of the Conservative party was maintained by those who were still to some extent oriented toward Great Britain. The new rulers of the Howe era inevitably backed the Liberal party; economic and political power were mutually dependent.

The old Conservative élite kept Diefenbaker from a central place in his party for many years. They ensured that the control of the party remained in Toronto. After Bennett's defeat in 1935, the Conservative party became a rump, with nearly all its strength in Ontario.[2]

2 This may seem to be contradicted by the leadership in those years being in the hands of Manion and Bracken. In both cases these men were the choices of the Toronto group. For example, Bracken was supported for the leadership against Murdo Macpherson because, in 1943, the CCF was a real threat in Ontario. It was hoped that by making a farmer head of the party, the rural ridings of Ontario would remain loyal provincially. Only with Drew did the Toronto group actually have one of its own.

Diefenbaker only came to leadership because of support from the fringe areas of the country, and because the Toronto group was at the end of its tether after the failure to build a national party under Drew. When, in 1957, Diefenbaker did squeeze in, he did so in spite of the dominant classes of the Howe era. Indeed, even after the business community had thrown over Bennett for King, it continued its contributions to the Conservative party, because it is wise for the wealthy to have their feet in both the opposition and the government. Despite these contributions, large-scale business did not expect or support the defeat of the Liberal party in 1957.

The cause of that defeat was a protest by Canadians not against the principles but against the pin-pricks of the Howe régime. The new engineers were not very agile in the legitimizing of power. In 1956, the Pipe-Line Debate was a signal example of failure to legitimize power. The Liberals openly announced that our resources were at the disposal of continental capitalism. The use of closure expressed the Howe administration's contempt for the "talking shop." So much did they identify their branch-plant society with the Kingdom of Heaven that they did not pay sufficient attention to the farmers or the outlying regions. Such regions existed for them as colonies of Montreal and Toronto. The Conservative victory was accomplished by local businessmen who felt excluded from their own country by corporation capitalism. Young men, ambitious for a life in politics, could not turn to the Liberal party, where the positions of power were well secured by the old pros. The Liberal's policy of satellite status to the United States, and their open attack on the British at the time of Suez, annoyed the residual loyalties of older Canadians.

Diefenbaker made the most of these pin-pricks in his campaign of 1957. The victory of 1958 followed as the night the day. The masses wanted a change. The business community naturally backed the successful. What did it have to fear when as orthodox a servant of business as Donald Fleming was given the finance portfolio in 1957? Quebec found it necessary to get on the bandwagon. Even Diefenbaker's nationalist rhetoric stirred the old memories. He was mistaken, however, when he imagined that such rhetoric was central to his victory. Later he was to rely on it, when it no longer brought the same response.

Within five years of gaining the largest majority in our history, Diefenbaker's government was defeated, and a new copy of the old régime was back in power. In this sense, at least, his administration had been a failure. Clearly he had not failed in sincerity, although the journalists of legitimacy even discounted that quality in him. They maintained that his nationalism was a cloak concealing the real man of ambition. But is it feasible to doubt his integrity at this point? In the Defence Crisis of 1963, his nationalism occasioned the strongest stand against satellite status that any Canadian government ever attempted. He maintained his stand even when the full power of the Canadian ruling class, the American government, and the military were brought against him. It is fair to maintain that such nationalism was misguided, but it is hardly honest to judge it to be insincere. What should be asked is: What kind of nationalism brought down on top of him the full wrath of a continental ruling class, and at the same time failed to produce feasible policies of government?

Diefenbaker saw his destiny as revivifying the Canadian nation. But what did he think that nation was? Certainly he had a profound – if romantic – sense of historical continuity. But a nation does not remain a nation only because it has roots in the past. Memory is never enough to guarantee that a nation can articulate itself in the present.[3] There must be a thrust of intention into the future. When the nation is the intimate neighbour of a dynamic empire, this necessity is even more obvious. Diefenbaker certainly saw his government as a spearhead of Canada's intention. His destiny was to revive a nation that had been disintegrating under the previous Liberal régime. Yet, because he was

3   National articulation is a process through which human beings form and re-form themselves into a society to act historically. This process coheres around the intention realized in the action. See Eric Voegelin, *The New Science of Politics* (Chicago: University of Chicago Press, 1952), pp. 37 *et seq.*

never specific about what Canada should be, he failed. In studying his government, one becomes aware of a series of mutually conflicting conceptions.

Diefenbaker was committed to a Canadian populism. He believed that he represented all the people and all the regions of the country. As a criminal lawyer he had learnt that the interests of the small need defending against the powerful. After 1958, he often repeated: "Everyone is against me but the people." One of his chosen models was Franklin Delano Roosevelt, and he interpreted Roosevelt's success as an appeal to the people over the heads of the great.

In the past, Diefenbaker's party had relied on support from the established classes in Ontario – from men whose philosophy was hardly that of the fair share. Diefenbaker contradicted his populism at the very beginning of his régime by appointing Donald Fleming the Minister of Finance. As an Ontario Tory, Fleming shared nationalism with Diefenbaker, but not populism. One of the comedies of this period was the tension between a Prime Minister set on populism and a Finance Minister who was even less Keynesian than Howe. It was ironic that Diefenbaker should have consented to a conversion loan that was obviously in the interest of the bond houses, while Fleming should have listened to his Prime Minister attacking the chartered banks over television. The tension between Diefenbaker and the business Conservatives was reconciled in the election of 1963. Nearly all the economic power deserted the Conservative party. He did not convince them with his nationalist appeals. The history of the breed does not make this surprising. The wealthy rarely maintain their nationalism when it is in conflict with the economic drive of the day.

By 1957, many Canadians could do with a spot of populism. The Howe-Abbott-Harris régime had run the country in the interests of Toronto-Montreal and their representatives in other provinces. The régime was building an expansionist society for the entrepreneur, the salesman, and the stock-broker. Diefenbaker's increased welfare payments and aid to "outlying regions" showed him turning to the people. But populist democracy is a dying force in contemporary

America. It belonged to the Saskatchewan or Wisconsin of Diefenbaker's youth, not to those who work for Simpson's-Sears or General Motors. When he combined his prairie populism with the private-enterprise ideology of the small town, it made a strange mixture. Diefenbaker, the foe of bureaucracy and planning, went ill with Diefenbaker, the admirer of Roosevelt. Nor did his talk of free enterprise belong to an older Canadian conservatism, which had used public power to achieve national purposes. The Conservative party had, after all, created Ontario Hydro, the CNR, the Bank of Canada, and the CBC.

Populism plus small-town free enterprise was entirely inadequate, and it could not come to terms with the society that had arisen since the war. Central Canada had grown into an industrialized complex. Any government to remain in office had to meet the new needs of this sector. A government set upon national revival had to do even more: it had to reverse the trend that was taking the keystone of the country and integrating it with Michigan and New York. Diefenbaker's administration did neither. He did not meet the needs of this heartland, and he realized no nationalist ends. His remarkable achievement was to alienate the support of both the rulers and the ruled in both Ontario and Quebec.

The Conservatives came to power at a time when world economics were less favourably disposed to Canada than at any time since the war. The less prosperous felt the pinches of the recession which started in 1957. Diefenbaker did not meet this situation with any co-ordinated economic plan. The government only alleviated the growing unemployment by winter works, and scarcely touched upon the problems caused by automation. Diefenbaker lost the wide support he had once held among the ordinary people of Ontario. Those who were suffering came to think his nationalism was the usual political yapping. Once more the Conservative party was associated with unemployment and recession.

At the same time, Diefenbaker succeeded in antagonizing the citadels of corporate power. His talk of free enterprise meant no more to corporate wealth than Barry Goldwater's did in 1964. During the Howe era, the wealthy had become used to running the country; they assumed it was natural there should be an identity of interests between themselves and the Liberal government. It is quite clear that this identity was far less complete under the Conservatives, despite Donald Fleming, than under the Liberals. The Conservatives handled the machine of state capitalism less skilfully than had the Liberal smoothies.

Not only did Diefenbaker lose political support in industrial Canada; he did not accomplish the work of economic nationalism. The "northern vision" was a pleasant extra, but no substitute for national survival. During his years in office, American control grew at a quickening rate. This was the crucial issue in 1957. If Canada was to survive, the cornerstone of its existence was the Great Lakes region. The population in that area was rushing toward cultural and economic integration with the United States. Any hope for a Canadian nation demanded some reversal of the process, and this could only be achieved through concentrated use of Ottawa's planning and control. After 1940, nationalism had to go hand in hand with some measure of socialism. Only nationalism could provide the political incentive for planning; only planning could restrain the victory of continentalism

Later I will argue that no such combination was possible, and therefore our nation was bound to disappear. To write of "ifs" in history is always foolish. Nevertheless, if Diefenbaker had been a realistic nationalist, he would have had to try some such policy. He would have had to appeal over the heads of corporation capitalism to the masses of Ontario and Quebec. He would have had to mobilize the electorate to support the use of Ottawa's power for nationalist purposes. Above all, he would have had to have known that the corporation élite was basically anti-national.

Perhaps a criminal lawyer who had spent his life between Prince Albert and Ottawa could remain unaware of what had happened in central Canada since 1940. After his sweeping. victory of 1958, Diefenbaker even seems to have thought that he had become a leader of "all the people," a conception that corporation capitalism could never take seriously. Had he forgotten why he had been kept by the traditional

Ontario classes from the leadership of his party for so long, and how he had come into power in 1957? Never in Canadian history had a party come to power with fewer debts to large business than in the election of 1957. But Diefenbaker seems to have been blinded into believing that the powerful of central Canada could still be appealed to as "my fellow Canadians," and were not committed to continentalism by the very nature of what they did. He seems to have been blinded into believing that "Canadianism" could provide the basis for a harmony of interests between his populist nationalism and the new central Canada. The Canada he thought about was not the country he was required to govern.

There is something naïve about Diefenbaker's attacks on Toronto and Montreal business in the 1963 election, particularly in the light of the economic policies his government had pursued from 1958 to 1962. It is not surprising that the only literate and established voice on the side of Diefenbaker in the election of 1963 was Senator Grattan O'Leary, who was himself caught in the trap of romantic nationalism. Senator O'Leary also was a supporter of both nationalism and capitalism. He could presumably combine the two because he thought the leaders of Canadian capitalism after 1940 were still nationalists. There seems less excuse for such nonsense from the publisher of a great eastern newspaper than from a western lawyer. It is, nevertheless, startling that the western lawyer could still believe capitalists were nationalists after a term as Prime Minister. In short, Diefenbaker did not understand the economic implications of Canadian nationalism; he could not appraise the class structure realistically, and therefore he could not formulate the economic policies that were necessary if nationalism was to be more than rhetoric and romance. Even after his defeat, he does not seem to have learnt these lessons. As Leader of the Opposition, he attacked the measures put forward by Walter Gordon to limit the control of this country by American capital.

Diefenbaker's confusion of populism, free enterprise, and nationalism can be seen in his dealings with James Coyne, the Governor of the Bank of Canada. Leaving aside the legal rights of the Bank or the behaviour of the Governor or the Government, it is clear that Coyne was a firm Canadian.[4] He advocated a "tight-money" nationalism that would protect Canada from foreign control. This may not have been the most effective protection, but it was at least one viable alternative. Diefenbaker rejected it. He also rejected the only other possible nationalist alternative – stringent governmental control of investment.

The free-enterprise assumptions of the Diefenbaker administration led to actions that were obviously anti-national. In appointing the Glassco Commission as an equivalent to the Hoover Commission, the government seemed to be appealing to an element of the American "conservative" tradition. The civil service was investigated by the head of Brazilian Traction. Although such "conservatism" may be appropriate to the United States, it cannot be to Canada, where limiting the civil service in the name of free enterprise simply strengthens the power of the private governments. Such strengthening must be anti-nationalist because the corporations are continental.

Diefenbaker's relations with the civil service invite the writing of a picaresque novel. By including these strained relations under his failures, I do not imply that the fault lay all on his side. Too many civil servants had too closely identified themselves with Liberal men and Liberal measures before 1957, and some of these did not show the proper loyalty to the elected government after 1957. Some of the senior civil servants were certain they knew what was best for Canada, both internally and externally, and they were not willing to accept the fact that elected leaders could sensibly advocate alternative policies. In the summer of 1963, the photograph of Pearson being welcomed back to office by the deputy ministers showed how far the British conception of the civil service had disappeared.[5] Nevertheless, that Diefenbaker failed

4   One complication was that Coyne came from an old Liberal family. The affair illustrated Diefenbaker's failure to forget old differences when great issues were at stake.

5   The question will be raised later whether the civil service could have been persuaded to co-operate with nationalist policies, or whether its leading personnel were too deeply involved with international administration.

to win the respect of the civil service was a disaster. No modern state can be run without great authority in the hands of its non-elected officials. In such an uncertain nation as Canada, the civil service is perhaps the essential instrument by which nationhood is preserved. The power of Ottawa has to be skilfully used by politicians to balance the enormous anti-national forces concentrated in the economic capitals of Toronto and Montreal. If Diefenbaker was to foster nationalism, he needed to win the respect of the civil service. The best civil servants were devoted to both the British account of their function and the conception of a sovereign Canadian nation. Only under Alvin Hamilton was a team of civil servants brought in to realize new goals.

It was from George Drew that Diefenbaker inherited the free-enterprise policy of limiting the crown corporations. The Conservatives had long supported the Canadian Pacific Airlines in Parliament. It soon became evident that their objections to the Pipeline had been only constitutional. They did not object to the control of public resources by private and foreign capitalists, but simply to the way Howe had pushed that control through Parliament. The administration's policy toward broadcasting is extraordinarily difficult to reconcile with any consistent nationalism. The Conservatives had long advocated a reassessment of broadcasting policy and the creation of a supervisory power to stand above both the CBC and the private broadcasters. For years Fleming had been advocating more power for private broadcasters, and he had gained support for his party when they really needed it. The Conservatives also justifiably felt that the CBC, then as today, gave too great prominence to the Liberal view of Canada. The broadcasting policy of the Conservatives was a compromise between various elements in the party. Diefenbaker and Nowlan restrained the Toronto Tories from an all-out attack on the CBC. But the Board of Broadcast Governors was implemented; a private television network was established; licences for television stations were ladled out to prosperous party supporters. Thus the Conservative party became identified with an attack on one of the central national institutions. It was forgotten that the CBC had been established by a Conservative government under Bennett, in order to maintain national control over broadcasting and to prevent the airwaves being used simply for private gain. The encouragement of private broadcasting must be anti-nationalist: the purpose of private broadcasting is to make money, and the easiest way to do this is to import canned American programs appealing to the lowest common denominator of the audience. Diefenbaker's policy was not even politically successful. John Bassett did not have the stuff of loyalty, and turned on Diefenbaker in 1963.

The most bewildering aspect of Diefenbaker's nationalism was his failure to find effective French-Canadian colleagues. The keystone of a Canadian nation is the French fact; the slightest knowledge of history makes this platitudinous. English-speaking Canadians who desire the survival of their nation have to co-operate with those who seek the continuance of Franco-American civilization. The failure of Diefenbaker to act on this maxim was his most tragic mistake. The election tactic of 1957, by which the Conservatives made no appeal to French Canada, helped to gain them an initial plurality. This may have been necessary after all the years of Liberal doubletalk. The cynical belief that Quebec would go along with the winning side proved correct in 1958. How, on so base a motive, did Diefenbaker expect to build a permanent loyalty to the Conservative cause among a sophisticated and threatened people? With fifty Quebec seats behind him from 1958 to 1962, Diefenbaker does not seem to have sought serious French lieu-tenants who could mediate the interests of their people to the rest of the country. He seems to have contented himself with the rag and bobtail of the *Union Nationale*. Despite present propaganda, there were noble elements in that party. Even after the death of Duplessis, in September of 1959, Diefenbaker does not seem to have tried to bring such obvious Quebec conservatives as Bertrand into his cabinet. Duplessis's death was followed immediately by that of his successor, J.M.P. Sauvé, in January of 1960. This was the deepest blow that Canadian conservatism ever sustained. Sauve could have become the first French-Canadian Conservative Prime Minister. However, this disaster need not have prevented Diefenbaker from seeking out other leaders from the *Union Nationale.*

There was one aspect of Diefenbaker's nationalism that was repugnant to thoughtful French Canadians, however attractive to English-speaking Liberals and New Canadians. He appealed to one united Canada, in which individuals would have equal rights irrespective of race and religion; there would be no first- and second-class citizens. As far as the civil rights of individuals are concerned, this is obviously an acceptable doctrine. Nevertheless, the rights of the individual do not encompass the rights of nations, liberal doctrine to the contrary. The French Canadians had entered Confederation not to protect the rights of the individual but the rights of a nation. They did not want to be swallowed up by that sea which Henri Bourassa had called *"l'américanisme saxonisant."* Diefenbaker's prairie experience had taught him to understand the rights of ethnic and religious communities, such as the Ukrainians and the Jews. He was no petty Anglo-Saxon homogenizer who wanted everybody to be the same. He had defended the rights of communities to protect their ancient cultural patterns. But in what way was this different from the United States, where Polish and Greek Americans keep their remembrances while accepting the general ends of the Republic? The French-Canadian nation, with its unique homeland and civilization, is quite a different case. The appeal of a nation within a nation is more substantial than that of the Ukrainians or the Jews. For Diefenbaker, the unity of all Canadians is a final fact. His interpretation of federalism is basically American. It could not encompass those who were concerned with being a nation, only those who wanted to preserve charming residual customs.

This failure to recognize the rights of French Canadians, *qua* community, was inconsistent with the roots of Canadian nationalism. One distinction between Canada and the United States has been the belief that Canada was predicated on the rights of nations as well as on the rights of individuals. American nationalism was, after all, founded on the civil rights of individuals in just as firm a way as the British appeal to liberty was founded on these rights. As the price of that liberty, American society has always demanded that all autonomous communities be swallowed up into the common culture. This was demanded during the Civil War; it was demanded of each immigrant; it is still the basis of the American school system. Diefenbaker appealed to a principle that was more American than Canadian. On this principle, the French Canadians might as well be asked to be homogenized straight into the American Republic. In so far as he did not distinguish between the rights of individuals and the rights of nations, Diefenbaker showed himself to be a liberal rather than a conservative.

To explain the failure of prairie nationalism to understand French Canada, I must turn to the older quarrels that have beset the nation. The two original peoples, French and Catholic, British and Protestant, united precariously in their desire not to be part of the great Republic; but their reasons were quite different. This union was precarious partly because the preponderant classes of British stock were determined that the Canadian nation should support the international policies of the British Empire, whereas the French were either indifferent or hostile to these policies. In the Boer War and the World War of 1914 and 1939, the English-speaking Canadians forced their determination on the French. Many of the Conservatives who came to power with Diefenbaker – Gordon Churchill, Alvin Hamilton, Douglas Harkness, George Pearkes, George Hees – were men of the 1939 war. They had taken many of their views of French Canada from their bitterness over the Conscription Crisis, in which Mackenzie King had seemed to support French isolationism. Diefenbaker and Howard Green were of the generation that had seen Canadian nationalism and proBritishness closely united. It was this that gave their nationalism some real bite in an era swamped by continentalism. It is well to remember that the anti-British nationalists of English-speaking Canada in the 1930's have nearly all shown the emptiness of their early protestations by becoming consistent continentalists later on. Nevertheless, the very tradition that bred so intense a nationalism in Diefenbaker and Green and Churchill inhibited them from coming to terms with French Canada and finding a base for the Conservative party in Quebec. In the Defence Election of 1963, it was a sad fact for Canadian nationalism that Green and Diefenbaker were unable to find any support for their policies in Quebec, although they were a government keeping nuclear arms off Canadian soil. By this stage in our history, Diefenbaker's and Green's nationalism was taking the form of a new kind of neutralism, a simple refusal to accept any demand from the present imperialism. It might have been thought that such a policy would have appealed to elements in Quebec. Indeed, to maintain such a policy Diefenbaker needed that support. It was not forthcoming. It was impossible for prairie nationalists and French-Canadian nationalists to get together. During the five years of his immense power, Diefenbaker had not encouraged French-Canadians to feel sympathy for the nationalism he advocated, and populism in Quebec had turned to the Social Credit movement. The very nature of Diefenbaker's Protestantism made him unsympathetic to Catholic Quebec. He even broke with tradition and did not appoint an Ontario Catholic to his Cabinet – this during a period when the Catholic population was a stronger force than ever before. Only after dissolution in 1963 did he appoint Frank McGee to his Cabinet.

Diefenbaker's nationalism included contempt for the intellectual community, particularly the one found in the universities. In the age and community in which he spiritually belonged, this would not have been an important failure. The universities had no great political place in the 1920's and 1930's; but in the 1950's and 1960's, they were playing a more public role. Both Roosevelt and Kennedy had found it useful to harness elements from the intellectual community to their administrations. Diefenbaker was unwise to treat the university community with the neglect and contempt that he did. To take one example – it is difficult to believe that the leading contemporary theorist of the conservative view of Canadian history, Professor D.G. Creighton, should never have been used on the manifold boards, councils, commissions, etc., that formulate our national policies. Not only was he the biographer of Diefenbaker's hero, Sir John A. Macdonald, but Creighton had defined the conservative view of Canada to a whole generation. He had the courage to do this when a definition of conservatism was not being welcomed by the Liberal establishment. Did not Diefenbaker know that the existence of Canada depended on a clear definition of conservatism? Did he not know that there had been diverse formulations of the meaning of Canadian history? For most of his appointments to Royal Commissions and other bodies, Diefenbaker chose the established wealthy or party wheelhorses. When he did choose from the university community, he turned to administrators and technicians, to those with the minimum of intellectual conviction. In the election of 1963, Diefenbaker had no support from the intellectual community, although he was standing on the attractive platform of Canadian sovereignty. This is a measure of how far he had carried yahooism in his years of office. He acted as if friendship with public-relations men and party journalists was a sufficient means to an intellectual nationalism.

Chapter Three

THE DEFENCE CRISIS of 1962 and 1963 revealed the depth of Diefenbaker's nationalism. Except for these events, one might interpret him as a romantic demagogue yearning for recognition. But his actions during the Defence Crisis make it clear that his nationalism was a deeply held principle for which he would fight with great courage and would sacrifice political advantage. Nothing in Diefenbaker's ministry was as noble as his leaving of it. The old war-horse would not budge from his principle: The government of the United States should not be allowed to force the Canadian government to a particular defence policy. His determination to stand on that belief finally convinced the ruling class that he was more than a nuisance, that he must be removed.

One comedy in these tragic events was that the intellectuals could not recognize that Diefenbaker was standing on principle. Such a recognition would have been outside the scope of the class-liberalism by which North-American intellectuals live. The literati had assessed Pearson to be the intellectual of principle who did not know the political arts, and Diefenbaker as the tough provincial politician interested in succeeding at all costs. Yet Diefenbaker was willing to bring the dominant classes of society down on his head; while Pearson changed his defence policies to suit the interests of the powerful. After the Cuban Crisis, Pearson acted with great political skill to unite the powerful forces of continentalism around him.

The crisis over defence blew into an issue after October of 1962, when Kennedy demanded that Castro's Cuba remove its missiles. A conflict had long been brewing between Howard Green, the Minister of External Affairs, and the military, whose spokesman in the Cabinet was

Douglas Harkness, the Minister of Defence. It was brought to a head over Cuba because it was rumoured that in the crisis between the United States and the USSR, the Canadian government had been slow in alerting Canadian forces involved in North-American defence. The facts of Canadian action in October of 1962 are still in dispute. It is certainly clear that influential sections of the Canadian military did not think that the government had properly acquiesced in NORAD. The issue soon rose to much greater proportions. Diefenbaker had buzzing around his ears the American government, the military, and soon the uproar of the Canadian power élite with its press. Under Pearson, the Liberal party became the spokesman of these forces. Whether Canada should arm the Bomarc missiles with atomic warheads became the issue at stake. Pearson, who had previously argued that Canada should not accept nuclear arms, turned round and asserted that any government of his would promptly negotiate their acceptance.

The crisis is illuminated by the forces that confronted Diefenbaker during those months. The Canadian head of a great American soap company first questioned publicly the government's relations with the United States. Hellyer and Pearson reversed the Liberal defence policy. The supreme Commander at NATO, General Norstad, gave a press conference in Ottawa under the auspices of the Canadian military, in which he implied that Canada was not living up to its commitments. The American State Department issued a memorandum denying the veracity of the Canadian Prime Minister on the matter. The three Toronto newspapers (two of them traditionally Conservative) came out on the same day for Diefenbaker's removal. Through all the abuse that Diefenbaker has suffered, he may well remember that it took the full weight of the North-American establishment to bring him down. He may well remember that, in the election of 1963, he still maintained nearly one hundred seats in Parliament when all the resources of the establishment were against him.

In the months of the crisis, there was a clear distinction between the motives of Green and Diefenbaker. They were old and trusted friends, deeply shaped by the same tradition of Canadian conservatism. Green had nominated Diefenbaker for the leadership of his party as long ago as 1948 when George Drew won the contest. When he became Minister of External Affairs in 1959, Green was clearly Diefenbaker's first lieutenant. In this office, his first consideration was that Canada's best role in international affairs should be to use its influence for disarmament. He believed that Canada's acquisition of nuclear arms would add to nuclear tension and diminish Canadian influence abroad. In all this he took for granted that there was such an entity as "Canada," that it was sufficiently a sovereign nation for this kind of policy to be possible.

During and after the Cuban Crisis, another factor came more to the fore. Green publicly questioned American actions around the world, not only in Laos and Vietnam. He went as far as to warn the Americans that their preponderant power might tempt them to be bullies. Indeed, in those months he expressed a deeper disquiet about the role of the United States in the world than any Canadian leader had done for generations. In Parliament, on January 24, 1963, he said:

> *The Cuban episode has made perfectly clear that in the world today the preponderance of power is with the United States. No longer is it a question of two great equal nuclear powers.*
>
> *I suggest that at the present time the United States is beyond any shadow of doubt preponderant in power. That, Mr. Chairman, may constitute quite a temptation. When you are the biggest fellow in the school yard it is quite a temptation to shove everybody else around. Now, I am confident that there will be no such development in United States policy. I am confident that they will not adopt a policy of getting tough with their allies. For Canada, of course, it is particularly important whether anything of that kind develops.*[6]

Whether he was wise to be so explicit depends on how one interprets the role of the United States in the world, and this question cannot be undertaken here. Suffice it to say that for those who accept Howard Green's interpretation, his actions during those months make him one

6 See *Hansard* of that date, p. 3067.

of the rare politicians who literally deserve the prefix "Right
Honourable." Whether wisely or not, Canada played a more independent role internationally during those short months than ever before in
its history. It was not likely that the American government under
Kennedy would take such talk lightly from its closest "ally." The gentler
régime of Eisenhower was a thing of the past. In 1962, Kennedy had
made clear that the United States was no longer going to take any
nonsense from its allies. An air of innocence pervades Green's statements about the United States. He spoke as if his comments would be
taken in friendship. He seemed unaware that he was an official in a
satellite country. Can an ant be an ally with an elephant?

Diefenbaker stood for a much more limited nationalism. He did not
criticize American world policy, but insisted that Canadian defence
policy should not be determined in Washington. Only at one point did
he by implication criticize American world policy. In calling for the UN
to investigate Cuba, he implied that he did not automatically accept
Kennedy's account of the facts. At no other time did he imply any
criticism of America's world role; he simply affirmed his belief in
Canadian sovereignty. In his speech to Parliament on February 5, 1963,
just before it voted down his government – surely a great document of
Canadian nationalism – he did not attack American policy even when
the weight of the American government was being used against him
through General Norstad's press conference and the press release on
Canadian relations by the American State Department.[7] Even during

7   On his first trip abroad, after his Inauguration in 1961, Kennedy had
    come to Ottawa and made a strong pitch for Canada's membership
    in the OAS, which was met without response from the Canadian
    government and Parliament. The President had also publicly
    announced that the United States was going to demand greater co-
    operation from its "allies," even if this meant less ease in friendship.
    In light of these events, it is surprising how Diefenbaker showed
    himself little ready for the great pressure that the American govern-
    ment would exert for the overthrow of his régime. Because of his
    early assassination, Kennedy's policy of exerting pressure on his
    "allies" only succeeded with two countries, Canada and the United
    Kingdom.

the following election, when he was under attack by such friends of the
Kennedys as the publisher of *Newsweek,* and when the Liberals had the
Kennedys' own election expert Louis Harris advising them, he refrained
from any attack on the aims of the American Empire. He continually
repeated that Canada should settle its defence commitments after the
facts were clarified by the NATO meetings in May of 1963. His opponents successfully raised the cry of "indecisiveness." (Decisiveness had
become a good slogan under the Kennedys.) They explained his actions
by saying that he was trying to have the best of Harkness's and Green's
positions for the low motive of political success. Such an explanation
cannot hold water for the simple reason that he was willing to let
Harkness go, and in doing so he must have known the price he was
paying. His speech at the dissolution of parliament made clear that the
one thing he would not stomach was the United States government
determining Canadian defence policy.

Diefenbaker and General Pearkes, the Defence Minister before
Harkness, had negotiated the acceptance of the Bomarcs when they
scrapped the Arrow program. The Bomarcs were useless without
nuclear warheads. It was claimed that in refusing the warheads
Diefenbaker was reneging on his own commitment to the United
States. It was even claimed that he might not have understood the
nature of the original commitment. In refusing to make up his mind
about accepting the warheads, he was accused of being "indecisive."
The "bad ally" and "the man of indecision" became Liberal images for
the campaign.

Diefenbaker answered these charges in his speech to Parliament on
January 25, 1963.[8] He claimed that the acceptance of warheads for the
Bomarcs had always been conditional on needing them for the defence
of the alliance. Defence technology was in constant flux, and it was no
longer clear that warheads were necessary. He maintained that the decision should await the NATO meetings in May of 1963, when there was to

8   It will be well for historians to read the *Hansard* of that day. By this
    stage in the crisis, the press was baying for Diefenbaker's blood, so
    the force of his arguments was not given much public prominence.

be an over-all assessment of the military needs of the alliance. The interests of world peace demanded that warheads should be kept off Canadian soil until it was certain that they were needed. This speech illuminates his assumptions about Canada's place in the world. He was no pacifist, no unilateralist, nor was he sentimental about Communism. If nuclear arms were necessary for North-American defence, Canada would take them. He also assumed that NATO was an alliance and not simply an American instrument. (After all, it was the Russians who had maintained the contrary for many years.) Canada's sovereignty entailed that our defence policy be determined in Ottawa. These last two assumptions did not correspond with reality and could not be politically sustained in the climate of Diefenbaker's own country.

How much was Diefenbaker aware that Canadian nationalism was no longer an effective rallying-cry in the urban Canada of 1963? Did a man with his past realize how much the structure of society had been changed in the Howe era so that the ruling class was no longer indigenous? Was he aware that a branch-plant society could not possibly show independence over an issue on which the American government was seriously determined? Most Canadians were as convinced as the American public that Kennedy had been right doing what he did in Cuba, and that his actions showed the wisdom of "decisiveness" in foreign policy. So "decisiveness" was subtly identified with Canada's need to have atomic arms.

Green's appeal to a gentler tradition of international morality had little attraction for the new Canada, outside of such unimportant groups as the Voice of Women. It seems likely that Diefenbaker actually believed that NATO was an alliance of sovereign states, not an instrument of the American Empire. Pearson had always acted internationally from different premises. His unequivocal praise of American action in Cuba showed that he knew there was a difference between Canadian initiative limiting the actions of a dying British power at the time of Suez and Canadian influence limiting the actions of the American Empire. He could use the rhetoric of "internationalism" even more effectively than Green, but he knew it for what it was.

Can it be denied that the actions of the Kennedy administration were directed toward removing an unreliable government in Ottawa rather than to guaranteeing a specific commitment? The American Secretary of Defense, Robert McNamara, made clear that the Bomarcs were not essential to the defence of North America. Diefenbaker and Green must have seemed too suspicious of American motives to be allowed to remain in office.[9] Their relation to the OAS and Cuba endangered what lay ahead in South America. Kennedy was a past master in the use of power for personal and imperial purposes. Historians will only be able to speculate about what Pearson and Kennedy discussed before the dinner for Nobel-Prize winners at the White House in 1962.

The Defence Crisis illustrated how profoundly Diefenbaker's Canadianism was bound up with the British connection. Since 1914, Britain had ceased to be a great power. Both Green and Diefenbaker continued to accept as real, however, the meaning of Canada's membership in the British Commonwealth. The character of Canada as British North America was in their flesh and bones. Yet it was their fate to be in charge of the Canadian government at the time that the English ruling class had come to think of its Commonwealth relations as a tiresome burden, when the wealthy of Canada had ceased to be connected with their British past. It is easy for the clever and the rootless to point out the mistakes that Diefenbaker and Green made in this regard; it is kinder, however, to sympathize with these men of deep loyalty, who found themselves impotent in the face of their disappearing past.

The British connection had been a source of Canadian nationalism. The west-east pull of trade – from the prairies, down the Great Lakes and the St. Lawrence, to western Europe – provided a counter-thrust to the pull of continentalism. It depended on the existence of a true North Atlantic triangle. But the Britishness of Canada was more than economic. It was a tradition that stood in firm opposition to the

9 In the election of 1963, American officials followed Green to his political meetings. It was innocent of Green to object to this. Did he not know how the CIA considered South American elections?

Jeffersonian liberalism so dominant in the United States.[10] By its nature this conservatism was not philosophically explicit, although it had shaped our institutions and had penetrated into the lives of generations of Canadians. Green and Diefenbaker were of this tradition. Such Canadians could not give their loyalty to the great Republic to the south. This did not imply anti-Americanism, simply a lack of Americanism. In the election of 1963, Diefenbaker was accused of anti-Americanism, but he was surely being honest to his own past when he said that he thought of his policies as being pro-Canadian, not anti-American. During the Howe era, this older Canadianism disappeared first in Toronto and Montreal, cities that once prided themselves on being most British. But ways of life die hard, and this loyalty still survived in the less modern parts of Canada. Loyalty cannot quickly be destroyed by economic circumstances because it does not depend on economics alone. In his speech at dissolution in 1963, Diefenbaker spoke with unerring historical appropriateness when he reminded his hearers of the Annexation Manifesto of 1849. The economic self-seekers had never been the ones to care about Canada as a nation.

With his passionate sense of British North America, Diefenbaker took office at a time when the Suez venture had driven home to the English their exact place in the world. The British decided then that their hope for any international influence lay in a careful manipulation of their "special" relation with the United States.[11] The loan that Keynes negotiated for them after 1945 guaranteed their being tied to the American Empire. Whether or not there was any alternative, they saw none. After all, their greatest contemporary leader, Churchill, had not de Gaulle's clarity of intelligence. Beginning in the 1960's, the United Kingdom decided to seek entrance to the new European community. They saw the

10 A discussion of British conservatism will be found later.

11 Bismarck said the central fact of the modern era was that the Americans spoke English. In 1917, the English brought in the Americans to settle their European quarrel. Thirty years later their ally had become their master.

European Common Market as an outreach of American power. They desired to free themselves as gracefully as possible from Commonwealth commitments. The length to which the English were willing to carry their "special" relation was seen in Lord Hume's trumpeting of support for American policy in Cuba, and Mr. Macmillan's ability to eat crow when the Americans cancelled the Skybolt program. As realistic a politician as de Gaulle graphically described the English as a Trojan Horse when he vetoed their entrance to Europe in January of 1963.

In this context, the appeal of the Conservatives to the British connection carried an air of unreality. The pattern of Canadian trade could not be changed in the way Diefenbaker suggested in 1957. He understood this himself by the time he turned down the United Kingdom's later proposals for a free-trade area with Canada. After such a refusal, the English could not stomach the appeal he made for the Commonwealth in London, in September of 1962. It seemed the stuff of fantasy, not a viable alternative. Tough politicians like Macmillan and Duncan Sandys were quick to use the press, and Diefenbaker was accused of trying to upset England's entry into the Common Market. Men who felt deeply about the Commonwealth could be accused of being bad allies, not only of the United States but also of the United Kingdom. The two had become synonymous, once the English had become a satellite. This was made crystal clear when Lord Home welcomed Pearson back to power as a "good ally" at the NATO meetings in Ottawa in May of 1963. Because the English had been rejected by the Europeans as an American Trojan Horse, they had little sympathy with such a peripheral matter as Canadian nationalism. After what the English did to him in 1962 and 1963, Diefenbaker still fought for the Red Ensign in 1964. His basic principles were far removed from any petty sense of self-importance.

It was often considered strange that a Conservative government should follow the independent internationalism associated with Green. The only explanation brought forward by its opponents was that the administration was overwhelmed with a pathological "indecision." But there was something consistent and inevitable in Green's policies.

Green and Diefenbaker had always considered Canada an independent country. The role of Canada was to mediate between the United States and western Europe, particularly Great Britain. But this conception could no longer fit the facts. By the 1950s NATO was a servant of the American Empire. The Canadian élite accepted the consequences of this for Canada. But Green could not accept the end of independence. He cried out against Canada becoming a vassal. As the Commonwealth had so little substance, the only role now possible seemed that of an independent agent in the United Nations, exerting influence for disarmament. His Protestant idealism pointed in the same direction. But such independence in international relations was not something the dominant forces in Canadian life could accept. The sincerity of Diefenbaker's nationalism is established by the fact that he stood by Green, and would not accept the American demands, even when it was in his overwhelming interest to do so. One is reminded of Milton's Abdiel: "Unshaken, unseduced, unterrified."

Chapter Four

IN THE LIGHT OF DIEFENBAKER, I would like to turn to the Canadian establishment and its political instrument, the Liberal party. There are three arguments for nationalism that could justify the Liberals. First, the Liberals are the realistic defenders of this country, piloting us through the shoals of foreign control and internal dissension that might shipwreck Canada. Second, in the twentieth century it is inevitable that Canada should be swallowed up; since 1940 this should have been obvious to any political analyst. Liberal leadership has recognized this and has taught the masses to accept it smoothly. Third, Canada's disappearance is not only necessary but good. As part of the great North American civilization, we enter wider horizons; Liberal policies are leading to a richer continentalism. The second and third arguments are often taken to be the same. They are identified because men assume in the age of progress that the broad movement of history is upward. Taken as a whole, what is bound to happen is bound also to be good. But this assumption is not self-evident. The fact that events happen does not imply that they are good. We understand this in the small events of personal life. We only forget it in the large events when we worship the future. The last two arguments for the Liberals are, therefore, clearly distinct.

The Liberals use the first of these three in public. There is still much nationalist sentiment in certain parts of the country. On the hustings the image of the Liberals has been that of the realistic defenders of Canadian unity. At the level of economic policy, the argument runs, they have shown themselves skilful masters of national development. This skill was exemplified in the policies of Howe from 1945 to 1957. These policies proceeded from the recognition of certain realities: that the Canadian economy was part of the total resources of North America; that Canada was an undeveloped frontier within that total, and the capital necessary for that development would come largely from the United States; that North America was committed to a capitalist structure in which the control of production would be in the hands of "private" corporations, while the government would only play a supervisory role.

Within these assumptions, the Liberal party gave brilliant leadership to the development of the country; the corporations ran an economy that was blessed by a benevolent government; certain complementary needs were met by the judicious use of Crown corporations; injustices were palliated with limited social services. If the terms for American investment had been tougher, there would have been less investment. Canada would have developed more slowly and with a substantially lower standard of living than the United States. This would have been the quickest way to undermine the nation. The inevitability of Howe's policies is seen by the fact that the Conservatives could find no viable alternative. Since coming back to office in 1963, the Liberals have recognized the need for a more nationalistic economic policy. Only the circumstances of minority government have prevented Walter Gordon from initiating it.

Beyond economic policy, the argument continues, the Liberals alone have understood that French Canada is the keystone of Confederation. They have always allowed for the legitimate interests of Quebec and have produced French leaders who supported Confederation. The provincial Liberal party has directed Quebec's awakening since Duplessis, and from 1963 the federal party has recognized that Quebec must have a new place in Confederation, if it is going to remain in the same country. Co-operative federalism is the only basis on which Quebec will stay. Pearson has wisely compromised with Prime Minister Lesage on matters of provincial autonomy. He has fought for a national flag free of any hated British symbols. He has established a strong Royal Commission on Bilingualism and Biculturalism. When one compares this with the previous administration, the claim of the Liberals is strong.

At the level of defence policy, the Liberals argue that the issue about
nuclear arms did not involve any surrender of proper Canadian sovereignty. Canada ought to play a fair and honourable part in "the defence
of the West," and the Americans are the leaders of that alliance. It is only
in terms of such realities that our nation can be built. Only as a friendly
satellite of the United States can we use such diplomats as Pearson to
influence the American leaders to play their world role with skill and
moderation. Doing this is not negating nationalism but recognizing its
limits. The Liberal argument was symbolized in August of 1963 when, on
the same weekend that the secret agreement with the United States over
nuclear warheads was announced, Pearson spoke feelingly about
Canadian nationalism at a meeting of Quebec journalists.

The whole argument for the Liberals as realistic nationalists breaks
down with their actual achievements. Their policies have not been such
as could sustain a continuing nation. The old adage "The operation
was a success but the patient died" can be too readily applied. They
were in office during the years when the possible basis for nationalism
disappeared. It was under a Liberal régime that Canada became a
branch-plant society; it was under Liberal leadership that our independence in defence and foreign affairs was finally broken. It is perfectly
convincing to argue that these policies were necessary for Canada or to
argue that they were good for Canada. The widespread claim that the
Liberals were the best possible régime is not the issue at this point. It
may be convincing to argue that if Howe had not existed, we would
have had to invent him. But it is absurd to argue that the Liberals have
been successful nationalists.

The Liberals failed in English-speaking Canada. If the nation were to
survive, it had to be anchored in both Englishand French-speaking
Canada, and a *modus vivendi* had to be established between the two.
The Liberals failed to recognize that the real danger to nationalism lay
in the incipient continentalism of English-speaking society, rather than
in any Quebec separatism. Their economic policies homogenized the
culture of Ontario with that of Michigan and New York.

The crucial years were those of the early forties. The decisions of those years were made once and for all, and were not compatible with the continuance of a sovereign Canadian nation.[12] Once it was decided that Canada was to be a branch-plant society of American capitalism, the issue of Canadian nationalism had been settled. The decision may or may not have been necessary; it may have been good or bad for Canada to be integrated into the international capitalism that has dominated the West since 1945. But certainly Canada could not exist as a nation when the chief end of the government's policy was the quickest integration into that complex. The Liberal policy under Howe was integration as fast as possible and at all costs. No other consideration was allowed to stand in the way. The society produced by such policies may reap enormous benefits, but it will not be a nation. Its culture will become the empire's to which it belongs. Branch-plant economies have branch-plant cultures. The O'Keefe Centre symbolizes Canada.

The Ontario vote in the national election of 1963 showed what that society had become. In the southern metropolitan areas, the writ of the continental corporations runs with small impediment, and the Liberals swept the board. A society dominated by corporations could not vote for an independent defence policy. The power of the American government to control Canada does not lie primarily in its ability to exert direct pressure; the power lies in the fact that the dominant classes in Canada see themselves at one with the continent on all essential matters. Dominant classes get the kind of government they want. The nature of our rulers was determined by the economic policies of the Liberals in the 1940's. The matter can be summed up quickly: The policies pursued by Howe produced a ruling class composed of such men

12 A note is required here about the use of such words as "decision" and "possible." In writing history one employs a certain logic, which one hopes has a high degree of consistency. For example, the use of the word "decisions" does not entail any concept of free will or imply that these "decisions" "could have been otherwise." It is clear that in this writing I am employing the word "fate" in a way that most modern writers avoid. They accept a modern notion of free will, while I accept a classical account of ethics. In this writing I cannot justify that vocabulary.

as E. P. Taylor. In the winter of 1963, Mr. Taylor was quoted as saying: "Canadian nationalism! How old-fashioned can you get?"

The democratic argument asserts that it took more votes than the votes of the powerful to make Pearson Prime Minister. Was it not the majority of Canadian people – and not simply the managers – that settled the issue? To meet this argument would require a long account of corporation capitalism and the processes whereby power is legitimized. This can obviously not be done in a short space. Let it suffice to make the following point: In no society is it possible for many men to live outside the dominant assumptions of their world for very long. Where can people learn independent views, when newspapers and television throw at them only processed opinions? In a society of large bureaucracies, power is legitimized by conscious and unconscious processes. The overwhelming vote for the Liberals in urban Ontario should not be surprising, since the powers of legitimacy were naturally strongest in those areas controlled by continental capitalism. The democratic idea of the free man making up his mind to create the society of his choice as he casts his ballot may have had meaning at some moments in history, but it can hardly apply in as dynamic a society as Southern Ontario. To say this is not to deny that the ballot box has ritual and other significance. A society proceeding from economic decisions made in the forties was not one capable of deciding on a defence policy or a foreign policy different from those of the United States or, for that matter, deciding on a distinct culture. Ontario was determined it would be integrated into the Great Lakes region.

It has been said that the inability of a country to have an independent foreign policy does not prevent it from being a nation. This means that Canadians have to recognize the limitations on sovereignty in a nation that lives beside the most powerful country on earth. This argument sees our case as similar to that of Poland. But whatever possible future there may be for Poland, there are clearly two chief differences between ourselves and that nation. First, the Poles have an ancient culture which has shown strength in resisting the new change. The new came to Poland not only as something Russian (that is, nationally alien) but also as something Marxist (that is, profoundly alien to a Roman Catholic people). In Canada outside of Quebec, there is no deeply rooted culture, and the new changes come in the form of an ideology (capitalist and liberal) which seems to many a splendid vision of human existence. Second, we are different from Poland in that in many ways capitalist imperialism is much harder to resist than Communist imperialism. This is not simply a matter of counting up the Hungarys and Tibets, the Brazils and Guatemalas, and seeing which empire has the lowest score. Nor is it simply that the United States is the most progressive society on earth and therefore the most radical force for the homogenizing of the world. By its very nature the capitalist system makes of national boundaries only matters of political formality. The governments of small capitalist nations do not have the same means to protect themselves as do small Communist states. Economic control is not finally in the hands of the government, and foreign capital is able to determine possible governments by incarnating itself as an indigenous ruling class. When Pearson praised Howe at the Liberal convention of 1958, he was surely showing that the existence of the Canadian nation was not a priority on the agenda of the Liberal party. The one implies the other.

Whether or not Pearson intended or recognized this implication is fundamentally unimportant. I do not wish to impugn the motives of the Liberal leaders. To understand public events, it is necessary to distinguish between "decision" and "intention." Intention, political or otherwise, is always hard to fathom. This does not prevent decisions made in public having consequences that are not difficult to understand. The "personalized" political journalism, associated on this continent with *Time* and exemplified in Canada by *Maclean's,* has done much to obscure this fundamental distinction. In the preceding arguments I am not concerned with the nature of intention, but with that of decision. It is therefore unnecessary to discuss whether those responsible were aware of the likely results of their decisions, or whether they thought these consequences good. For example, nothing that has been said implies that Pearson or his lieutenant, Jack Pickersgill, did not think of themselves as nationalists. To speculate about the intentions of those who were responsible for these decisions would require a series of biographies. One man might be described as believing in continentalism but as using the rhetoric of nationalism as the necessary cloak of the politician; another might be explained to be a nationalist who nevertheless could not bear to be out of office; a third might be a nationalist who did not understand the consequences of what he voted for in Cabinet. The results would not much affect the issues. The consequences of decisions can be understood historically for what they are, whereas the motives of the decision-makers are mainly of biographical – and perhaps of eternal – significance. Biography is not the purpose of this writing. The assertion that the Liberals were not successful nationalists does not depend on any assessment of their characters.[13]

The second way to justify the Liberals is to argue that politics is the art of leading people to accept necessities. As the argument goes, it was necessary for Canada to become part of the civilization of the United States. The Liberals have been the smooth instrument of that necessity. The last part of this argument has already been accepted – Liberal policies have led efficiently in that direction. Their record of smoothness is marred by their defeat in 1957. But they have quickly and efficiently regained power. The argument then turns on the truth of its first proposition, whether or not it was necessary for Canada to become part of the homogenized continental culture. And this in turn hinges on the question whether there were any possible alternatives to the decisions taken in the 1940's. If there were none, the necessity of Canada's disappearance is plain, and the argument in favour of the Liberal party follows.

13 The large amount of biographical writing about Mackenzie King in the last decade has done little to elucidate to what degree he was a nationalist, a continentalist, a man chiefly concerned about office, or a subtle conglomeration of all three, held together by his belief that a brilliant manipulation of day-to-day events was in his ordained hands sufficient to bring about the best of all possible worlds. King's biographers have failed to elucidate his intentions, partly because they did not understand what Marx and Freud have taught us about the logic of "intention."

What would these alternative policies have been? Nations must resist the capitalist and Communist empires in different ways. Resistance to western imperialism has taken two main forms. The first is to establish a rigorous socialist state that turns to the Communist empire for support in maintaining itself. This policy can be called Castroism after its most successful practitioner. The second method is to harness the nationalist spirit to technological planning and to insist internationally that there are limits to the western "alliance." This policy may be called Gaullism after its most successful practitioner.

Castroism was so obviously not a possible policy for Canada in the middle forties that it is hardly worth making the point that it was not. "Leftist" nationalism is only possible in a less-developed society in which the majority of citizens desires industrialism and believes that this is being prevented by anti-nationalist forces from the capitalist empire. This was not the situation in Canada.[14] Was there the possibility of some form of Gaullism in which the planning and control of investment would have left the ordering of the economy in Canadian hands? Gaullism is only possible when nationalism is such a dominant motive among certain élites that they are able to control the economy so as to stop the tendency of capitalism to become international. There are no such élites in the Canada of 1965.

In an earlier era, Macdonald's "National Policy" was of the Gaullist kind. It was possible because enough Canadians were determined to pay the economic price for such nationalism, and because Britain was still a dominant force pulling the flow of trade eastward. Enough entre-

---

14 Could Canada have achieved even the degree of independence that Mexico has maintained? This is not the place to compare the complex differences between the two countries. The conflict between the Spanish and the Indian in Mexico allowed the country to fit incomparably less easily into the common western pattern. Can one imagine Canadians expropriating the oil properties and taking on international capitalism as Cardenas did in the 1930s? Even with these traditions, it would seem likely that as Mexico is industrialized, its new middle class will make it an increasingly acquiescent neighbour.

preneurs could resist the pull of continentalism. Since R. B. Bennett's abortive social legislation of the late thirties, and the acquiescence of the succeeding Liberal government, the business community (particularly in Montreal, which was then more important than Toronto) has identified its interests with the Liberal party. This was Mackenzie King's chief political achievement. The organization of the war and of postwar reconstruction was carried on within the assumption that government action never questioned the ultimate authority of business interests to run the economy. Howe's cost-plus arrangements for war production make this clear. The Liberal politicians and civil servants always acted within that assumption because they knew their limited power depended on it. No government that acted on other principles would have lasted long. And to repeat, after 1940 it was not in the interests of the economically powerful to be nationalists. Most of them made more money by being the representatives of American capitalism and setting up the branch plants. No class in Canada more welcomed the American managers than the established wealthy of Montreal and Toronto, who had once seen themselves the pillars of Canada. Nor should this be surprising. Capitalism is, after all, a way of life based on the principle that the most important activity is profit-making. That activity led the wealthy in the direction of continentalism. They lost nothing essential to the principle of their lives in losing their country. It is this very fact that has made capitalism the great solvent of all tradition in the modern era. When everything is made relative to profit-making, all traditions of virtue are dissolved, including that aspect of virtue known as love of country. This is why liberalism is the perfect ideology for capitalism. It demolishes those taboos that restrain expansion. Even the finest talk about internationalism opens markets for the powerful.

If there had been an influential group that seriously desired the continuance of the country after 1940, it would have needed the animation of some political creed that differed from the capitalist liberalism of the United States. Only then could they have acted with sufficient decision to build an alternative nation on this continent. De Gaulle has been able to count on a deeply felt nationalism. This is based on a tradition that pre-dates the age of progress and yet is held by men who can handle the modern world. But no such tradition existed among any of the important decision-makers in Canada. The only Canadians who had a profoundly different tradition from capitalist liberalism were the French Canadians, and they were not generally taken into decision-making unless they had foregone these traditions. Their very Catholicism did not lead the best of them to be interested in the managerial, financial, and technical skills of the age of progress.

The only possible basis for a Gaullist élite would have been the senior civil servants working closely with politicians who knew what they were doing. Such a union of civil servants and politicians could have used the power of Ottawa to control the representatives of continentalism in Toronto and Montreal. In fact, the Liberal politicians and their civil servants saw themselves in pleasant co-operation with the tycoons of the real capitals. I must repeat again Mackenzie King's great discovery: If his government was the friend of business, the Liberal party could stay in office almost indefinitely. His chosen representative for that co-operation was C. D. Howe. An old newspaper photograph lingers in the mind. In the summer of 1945, a crowd of strikers followed Howe to a Toronto golf club. They had not been allowed to reach the Minister of Trade and Commerce officially. He was forced to speak with the unionists to get them out of the locker room. In his anger at the invasion of the country club, Howe made perfectly plain what post-war reconstruction would be like. The continental corporations were going to rule. Such Liberal politicians as Brooke Claxton and Paul Martin knew where the real power lay – in St. James and Bay Streets. They did not risk using the government as a nationalist instrument. The politicians, the businessmen, and the civil servants worked harmoniously together. The enormous majorities for the Liberals in 1945, 1948, and 1953 showed that the Canadian people were attuned to the system produced by this co-operation.

Any desire for nationalism among the civil service could not be effective. Some of them who directly served Howe, like Mitchell Sharp and William Bennett, obviously welcomed the union between government and international business. When they were forced out of the government by the Conservatives in 1958, they quickly found high places in international companies. But what of the traditional civil servants in the Departments of Finance and External Affairs? They had given their lives to government service and presumably wanted to serve a sovereign Canada. For over a generation, choruses of praise have been offered to these civil servants. How wonderful for Canada that it should be represented by such permanent officials as Norman Robertson and Robert Bryce. They have been spoken of as a kind of secular priesthood. Yet the country they represented is now a fragmented nation, a satellite.

It would be a travesty to deny that most of them wanted to preserve their country. But they were not of the diamond stuff of which nationalists must be made in these circumstances. Their education was not of a kind to produce a realistic attitude toward the twentieth century. The officials of the Department of Finance had mostly learnt their economics at Queen's University in Ontario, where the glories of the free market were the first dogma. But nationalism was negated by the policies that proceeded from such a dogma. The officials of External Affairs had mostly been educated in the twilight scepticism of Oxford liberalism. This kind of culture does not give one the stamina to be a nationalist in the twentieth century. They went on representing Canada at significant conferences, while the "new" Canada was being shaped by other hands in Southern Ontario. The old-fashioned city of Ottawa continued to shelter them from the Canada they had helped to make. They were not in a position to be the necessary nationalist élite. But where else could it come from? Isolated intellectuals in the universities? Small-town politicians who remembered?

Nevertheless it is interesting to speculate why the civil service élite did so little. To take the example of one government department, it seems likely that some officials in External Affairs have some feeling for the continuance of their nation. Yet they were the instruments of a policy that left Canada a satellite internationally. In 1940, it was necessary for Canada to throw in her lot with continental defence. The whole of Eurasia might have fallen into the hands of Germany and Japan. The British Empire was collapsing once and for all as an international force. Canada and the United States of America had to be unequivocally united for the defence of this hemisphere. But it is surprising how little the politicians and officials seem to have realized that this new situation would have to be manipulated with great wisdom if any Canadian independence was to survive. Perhaps nothing could have been done; perhaps the collapse of nineteenth-century Europe automatically entailed the collapse of Canada. Nevertheless, it is extraordinary that King and his associates in External Affairs did not seem to recognize the perilous situation that the new circumstances entailed. In all eras, wise politicians have to play a balancing game. How little the American alliance was balanced by any defence of national independence!

In the case of King, this lack of balance seems to be bound up with a very usual syndrome among people who give themselves to the practical life: when they gain power they carry on with the ideas they learnt thirty years before. King had seen the centre of Canadian independence as being threatened by the British; he had been raised by a beloved mother who was impregnated with the memory of the supposed injustices that her father, William Lyon Mackenzie, had received at the hands of the British. Even after 1940, he still held the fear that Canadian independence was threatened from Whitehall. It may also have been that King was sufficiently held by liberal theory to believe that the United States was a democracy, and therefore not in essence an imperial power like the old societies of Europe. His relations with the Rockefellers were certainly a classic case of the ability of liberals to fool themselves about the relation between capitalism and democracy. King seems to have admired instinctively the liberal rhetoric of Franklin Delano Roosevelt, and Roosevelt surely stands as a perfect example of the division between ideology and action. One of the great imperialists of American history imagined himself an enemy of imperialism.

In the late forties, NATO policy seems to have been advocated by senior civil servants not only as defence against the Russian Empire but also as a means of building an Atlantic community that would provide tugs on Canada other than the continental. Yet by the 1960's, NATO had become the military instrument of the strongest empire on earth. It may indeed be argued that the safety of the western world against the hostile forces of Asia requires that we be part of a tightly unified empire; the integration of Canada into that empire would be a small price to pay. Yet as realistic a politician as de Gaulle recognizes that he must try to limit the power of NATO if the existence of France as a country is to be maintained. American hegemony was obvious. Why was it not balanced by a greater initiative for independence? In the Defence Crisis of 1963, Green and Diefenbaker did not receive loyalty from their civil service. General Norstad's press conference in Ottawa in January of 1963 could hardly have been organized without help – the help of various top officials in the very government that held the policies that Norstad's remarks were undermining. Presumably the permanent officials felt justified in this action because their view of Canada was entirely dominated by the concept of "the good ally."

What seems central to this process is that such officials had in the previous twenty years become more and more representative of a western empire rather than civil servants of a particular nation state. They were part of an international bureaucracy, mainly English-speaking, whose chief job was to see that the West maintained its superior power over the East. They identified themselves with the international community rather than with nationalist "hayseeds" such as Green and Diefenbaker. In the final analysis, they were provincial servants of the greatest empire since Rome. Was there anything that could have been done to preserve Canadian independence after 1960? Where were the people in Canada who could have done it?

Chapter Five

THE CONFUSED STRIVINGS of politicians, businessmen, and civil servants cannot alone account for Canada's collapse. This stems from the very character of the modern era.[15] The aspirations of progress have made Canada redundant. The universal and homogeneous state is the pinnacle of political striving. "Universal" implies a world-wide state, which would eliminate the curse of war among nations; "homogeneous" means that all men would be equal, and war among classes would be eliminated. The masses and the philosophers have both agreed that this universal and egalitarian society is the goal of historical striving. It gives content to the rhetoric of both Communists and capitalists. This state will be achieved by means of modern science – a science that leads to the conquest of nature. Today scientists master not only non-human nature, but human nature itself. Particularly in America, scientists concern themselves with the control of heredity, the human mind, and society. Their victories in biochemistry and psychology will give the politicians a prodigious power to universalize and homogenize. Since 1945, the world-wide and uniform society is no longer a distant dream but a close possibility. Man will conquer man and perfect himself.

Modern civilization makes all local cultures anachronistic. Where modern science has achieved its mastery, there is no place for local

15 In what follows I use "modern" to describe the civilization of the age of progress. This civilization arose in Western Europe and is now conquering the whole globe and perhaps other parts of the universe. "Modern" is applied to political philosophy to distinguish the thought of Western Europe from that of the antique world of Greece.

cultures. It has often been argued that geography and language caused
Canada's defeat. But behind these there is a necessity that is incomparably more powerful. Our culture floundered on the aspirations of the
age of progress. The argument that Canada, a local culture, must disappear can, therefore, be stated in three steps. First, men everywhere
move ineluctably toward membership in the universal and homogeneous state. Second, Canadians live next to a society that is the heart of
modernity. Third, nearly all Canadians think that modernity is good, so
nothing essential distinguishes Canadians from Americans. When they
oblate themselves before "the American way of life," they offer themselves on the altar of the reigning Western goddess. When Pearson set
out on his electoral campaign of 1963, he was photographed reading
Will Durant's *The Dawning of the Age of Reason*. To Durant, the age of
reason is the age of progress. The book was therefore appropriate reading for Pearson, who was about to persuade Canadians to adopt
American atomic arms.

There are many who would deny the second statement in the previous paragraph, that the United States is the spearhead of progress.
Strangely enough, the two groups that deny it do so from opposite
positions. The Marxists deny it from progressive assumptions, and
American "conservatives" deny it because they consider their country
the chief guardian of Western values. These two points of view are
sometimes confused and combined by certain Europeans whose jeal-
ousy of the United States leads them to accuse Americans of being too
reactionary and too modern at one and the same time. To maintain my
stand that the United States is the spearhead of progress, these two
denials must be refuted. To do so, I must turn away from Canadian
history to the more important questions of modern political theory.

Marxists believe that their philosophy leads to the true understanding of history. They insist that the aims of the United States are hostile
to the interests of developing humanity. They assert that American
corporation capitalism – its system of property relations and conse-
quent world policies – makes the United States an essentially "reactionary" rather than a "progressive" force. The Russian and Chinese

leaders may disagree on how to deal with this situation, but they do not disagree about the diagnosis. Canadian Marxists have therefore argued that Canadian nationalism serves the interests of progress because our incorporation in the United States would add to the power of reaction in the world. To be progressive in Canada is to be nationalistic. To see where the Marxists are wrong in detail about Canada, I must discuss where they are wrong about the age of progress in general.

Marx believed that history unfolds as progress, and that when man's control of nature has eliminated scarcity, the objective conditions will be present for a society in which human beings no longer exploit each other. With the end of exploitation, men will not be alienated from their own happiness or from each other. A society will emerge in which the full claims of personal freedom and social order will be reconciled, because the essential cause of conflict between men will have been overcome. This world-wide society will be one in which all human beings can at last realize their happiness in the world without the necessity of lessening that of others. This doctrine implies that there are ways of life in which men are fulfilled and others in which they are not. How else could Marx distinguish between man's alienation and its opposite? Marxism includes therefore a doctrine of human good (call it, if you will, happiness). Technological development is a means by which all men will realize this good. But such a doctrine of good means that Marx is not purely a philosopher of the age of progress; he is rooted in the teleological philosophy that pre-dates the age of progress. It is the very signature of modern man to deny reality to any conception of good that imposes limits on human freedom. To modern political theory, man's essence is his freedom. Nothing must stand in the way of our absolute freedom to create the world as we want it. There must be no conceptions of good that put limitations on human action. This definition of man as freedom constitutes the heart of the age of progress. The doctrine of progress is not, as Marx believed, the perfectibility of man, but an open-ended progression in which men will be endlessly free to make the world as they want it. In Marxism, technology remains an instrument that serves human good. But many technologists speak as if mastery were an end in itself. To conquer space it may be necessary to transcend ordinary humanity, and produce creatures half flesh and half metal.

North-American liberalism expresses the belief in open-ended progress more accurately than Marxism. It understands more fully the implications of man's essence being his freedom. As liberals become more and more aware of the implications of their own doctrine, they recognize that no appeal to human good, now or in the future, must be allowed to limit their freedom to make the world as they choose. Social order is a man-made convenience, and its only purpose is to increase freedom. What matters is that men shall be able to do what they want, when they want. The logic of this liberalism makes the distinction between judgements of fact and judgements of value. "Value judgements" are subjective. In other words, man in his freedom creates the valuable. The human good is what we choose for our good.

In an earlier generation, liberals such as John Dewey claimed that this doctrine improved upon the past because it guaranteed a society in which all could do what they wanted, in which the standards of some would not be imposed upon others. Tastes are different, and we should have a society that caters to the plurality of tastes. How much fairer this would be than the old societies in which standards of virtue were imposed on the masses by pertinacious priests and arrogant philosophers. But this is not what is happening in our state capitalism. In the private spheres, all kinds of tastes are allowed. Nobody minds very much if we prefer women or dogs or boys, as long as we cause no public inconvenience. But in the public sphere, such pluralism of taste is not permitted. The conquest of human and nonhuman nature becomes the only public value. As this planet becomes crowded and even dangerous, our greatest public activity becomes "the exploitation of the solar system." The vaunted freedom of the individual to choose becomes either the necessity of finding one's role in the public engineering or the necessity of retreating into the privacy of pleasure.

Liberalism is the fitting ideology for a society directed toward these ends. It denies unequivocally that there are any given restraints that might hinder pursuit of dynamic dominance. In political terms, liberalism is now an appeal for "the end of ideology." This means that we must experiment in shaping society unhindered by any preconceived notions of good. "The end of ideology" is the perfect slogan for men who want to do what they want. Liberalism is, then, the faith that can understand progress as an extension into the unlimited possibility of the future. It does this much better than Marxism, which still blocks progress by its old-fashioned ideas of the perfectibility of man.

Marxists fail to understand the modern age when they assume that socialism is a more progressive form of organization than state capitalism. Implied in the progressive idea of freedom is the belief that men should emancipate their passions. When men are free to do what they want, all will be well because the liberated desires will be socially creative. This belief lies at the very centre of liberal movements.[16] Marx claimed to be the inheritor of the noblest aspects of liberal thought. He believed that when scientists had eliminated scarcity as the cause of greed and oppression, a society would arise in which the freedom of each to pursue his desires would not conflict with a happy social order. The dictatorship of the proletariat was a passing necessity that would lead into a society of freedom. Under Communism, the passions would be emancipated, but they would be socially useful, not the corrupt passion of greed caused by scarcity. Even those socialists who did not follow Marx in the doctrine of the withering away of the state still generally believed that socialism would create a society of freedom in the sense of the emancipated passions. Socialism was considered an essentially progressive doctrine. It led to freedom.

There is confusion in the minds of those who believe in socialism and the emancipation of the passions. It is surely difficult to deny that greed in some form is a desire that belongs to man *qua* man, and is not simply produced by the society of scarcity. If this is so, to emancipate the passions is to emancipate greed. Yet what is socialism, if it is not the use

16 This last doctrine reminds one of the vast gulf that separates modern moral philosophy from the central teachings of the antique world.

of the government to restrain greed in the name of social good? In actual practice, socialism has always had to advocate inhibition in this respect. In doing so, was it not appealing to the conservative idea of social order against the liberal idea of freedom? Even if socialists maintain that their policies would lead in the long run to a society of unrestricted freedom, in the short run they have always been advocates of greater control over freedom. This confusion in their thought is the chief reason why socialism has not succeeded in the large technological societies since 1945. Western civilization was committed in its heart to the religion of progress and the emancipated passions. Those who accepted such a doctrine found corporation capitalism was a much more suitable régime than the inhibiting policies of socialism.[17] Since 1945, Marxist socialism has had its triumphs, but these have been in authoritarian régimes, in societies that needed the discipline of authority in order to industrialize quickly. The triumphs have not been in the West.

Early capitalism was full of moral restraints. The Protestant ethic inhibited any passion that did not encourage acquisition. The greed of each would lead to the greatest good for all. But in the age of high technology, the new capitalism can allow all passions to flourish along with greed. *Playboy* illustrates the fact that the young executive is not expected to be Horatio Alger. The titillation of the jaded tastes of the masses serves the purpose of the corporation élites, so long as a sufficient quota of the young is siphoned off as scientists and executives. With automation, the work-ethic of Protestantism disappears. Liberal ideology reconciles the political power of the élites with the private satisfactions of the masses. State capitalism and liberalism are much more advanced manifestations of the age of progress than the Russian system with its official Marxism.

American conservatives also claim that the United States is not the most progressive society on earth. Conservatives maintain that American society retains certain traditional values that have been lost in

17 This failure of socialism to recognize itself as an essentially conservative force has nowhere been so patently obvious as in the confusions of the Canadian socialist movement.

Communist societies. This claim appeals to history by asserting that the American Revolution was essentially conservative – as distinct from the radical revolution in France. The American Revolution did not appeal to the perfectibility of man but to the traditional rights of Englishmen. At its heart there were the ideals of a constitutional government and the inalienable rights of persons and their property. It is admitted in such arguments that many who supported the revolution were influenced by French revolutionary ideas; but at the centre of the Republic were such men as Washington, Madison, Hamilton, and Adams, rather than such men as Jefferson and Paine. Edmund Burke castigated the revolution in France while he defended the American cause. This indicates the conservatism of the American Revolution. The claim of conservatives is that bourgeois constitutionalism has remained the dominant tradition of the Republic despite the continuing liberal attack.

This argument has at its heart an interpretation of the history of political philosophy with which the present writer would agree. To put that interpretation simply, modern political philosophy may be divided into two main waves.[18] The first wave started with Machiavelli and Hobbes and found its bourgeois expression in such British thinkers as Locke, Smith, and Hume. The chief originator of the second wave was Rousseau, and this wave has spread out into the world through Kant and Hegel. The earlier thinkers criticized the classical view of nature and natural law, but they still maintained some conception of what was natural. While believing that man's essence was his freedom, the later thinkers advocated the progressive mastery through that freedom of human and non-human nature. Man in his freedom was thought to stand outside nature, and therefore to be able to perfect it. We could interfere with nature and make it what we wanted. It is from this doctrine that the continuous revolution of the modern era has proceeded.

In applying this interpretation, the American conservatives claim that the United States was founded on the thought of the first wave,

18 For this account of political philosophy see Leo Strauss *Natural Right and History* (Chicago: University of Chicago Press, 1953).

while the Communist empires took their ideology from Rousseau and
Marx. Therefore the United States should be called a conservative force.
The founders of the American Republic were followers of Locke.[19] The
assumptions of Locke and Smith are said to have given English-speaking societies stability of constitutional government and freedom from
continuous revolution. They escaped the worst results of totalitarian-
ism (call it, if you will, totalitarian democracy) which swept eastward
from the continent of Europe. The capitalism of the English-speaking
world was stabilized by being founded on a conception of human
nature. The doctrine of human nature of Locke and Smith may be
inadequate compared to the classical teachings, but it is less destructive
of humanity than the later doctrines, which assert that men are
completely malleable to perpetual conditioning. Because of the conservative nature of the United States, as against the revolutionary character of the Communist empires, Christianity and Judaism have been able
to survive in North America, while they are persecuted in the modern
empires of the East. Whatever the imperfections of American
govermnent, it remains at least formally constitutional, while the
Marxist societies are tyrannies. The United States must be accepted as
the guardian of Western values against the perversions of Western revolutionary thought as they have spread into the East.

19 A recent Roman Catholic form of the argument from Locke makes an
    even fuller claim. It identifies the Lockian thoughts of the nation's
    founders with the political philosophy of Aquinas. Father Courtney
    Murray has made the same attempt for the United States that Acton
    made a century ago in England – the identification of the modern
    belief in political freedom with Catholic Christianity. Suffice it to say
    that Locke largely accepted Hobbes's account of the state of nature,
    while Aquinas accepted the Aristotelian account. How then can their
    doctrines of natural right be closely identified? Those who make such
    attempts should surely be asked to read Coleridge's writings on
    Locke. To find any close identification between Aquinas's and Locke's
    doctrines of the virtues surely requires a looser reading of both than
    nationalist prejudice and flattery of the spirit of the age should allow.
    This branch of Roman Catholic American political philosophy is
    hardly then to be treated seriously.

It is important to point out one effect of this argument on Canada and the United Kingdom. This appeal to Lockian liberalism has been the philosophy of those who have believed that English-speaking unity was the hope of the modern world. The basic assumption of Churchill's life was that the British future lay in its alliance with the United States – the unity of the democratic-capitalist nations.[20] In Canada, this appeal to English-speaking unity has also been used as an argument for the destruction of Canadian independence. In the events around which this writing turns, many conservative Canadians were convinced that Diefenbaker was being false to English-speaking unity in refusing nuclear arms. The Liberal victory was welcomed in the press of the United Kingdom, and Pearson has always appealed to those in England whose hopes lay in the special relation with the United States. Yet it must be pointed out that the argument from English-speaking unity must play an ambiguous role in relation to Canadian nationalism. If Lockian liberalism is the conservatism of the English-speaking peoples, what was there in British conservatism that was not present in the bourgeois thought of Hamilton and Madison? If there was nothing, then the acts of the Loyalists are deprived of all moral significance. Many of the American Tories were Anglicans and knew well that in opposing the revolution they were opposing Locke. They appealed to the older political philosophy of Richard Hooker. They were not, as the liberal Canadian historians have often described them, a mixture of selfish and unfortunate men who chose the wrong side. If there was nothing valuable in the founders of English-speaking Canada, what makes it valuable for Canadians to continue as a nation today?

To return to the general argument. There is some truth in the claim of American conservatives. Their society does preserve constitutional government and respect for the legal rights of individuals in a way that the eastern tyrannies do not. The perpetuation of these depends on the continuing tradition of Lockian liberalism among influential classes.

20 Many contemporary English Conservative leaders – Churchill, Macmillan, Hogg, and others – have been born of wealthy American mothers.

Bourgeois Protestantism, with its Catholic and Jewish imitations, have survived in the United States and give some sense of the eternal to many people. Nevertheless, these traditions – no longer the heart of American civilization – become more residual every year. Sceptical liberalism becomes increasingly the dominant ideology of those who shape society; and, as it was argued earlier, this ideology is the extreme form of progressive modernity. The United States is no longer a society of small property owners, but of massive private and public corporations. Such organizations work with the scientists in their efforts to master nature and reshape humanity. Internationally, the imperial power of these corporations has destroyed indigenous cultures in every corner of the globe. Communist imperialism is more brutally immediate, but American capitalism has shown itself more subtly able to dissolve indigenous societies. This can make it harder to resist than the blatant thrusts of the Russians or the Chinese. The new methods the social sciences use to dissolve the opposition in friendly or enemy societies are welcomed by the government of the United States.[21]

The history of how modern liberalism has replaced the older republican traditions cannot be given in detail. It is not surprising that this should have happened. It was in the West the idea arose that human nature is completely malleable, and this the United States today inherits. American society has also inherited the older aspects of the Western tradition: the Church, constitutional government, classical and philosophical studies. But every day these become more like museum pieces, mere survivals on the periphery.

The Americans who call themselves "Conservatives" have the right to the title only in a particular sense. In fact, they are old-fashioned liberals. They stand for the freedom of the individual to use his property as he wishes, and for a limited government which must keep out of the marketplace. Their concentration on freedom from governmental interference has more to do with nineteenth-century liberalism than

21 See "Toward a Technology of Human Behaviour for Defense Use" by Charles W. Bray, in *The American Psychologist* (August 1962). This is a synopsis of a report to the American Secretary of Defense.

with traditional conservatism, which asserts the right of the community to restrain freedom in the name of the common good. Senator Goldwater appealed directly to the American Constitution and to Locke, its philosophical architect. The Senator's chief economic adviser, Professor Milton Friedman, appeals to the British liberal economists of the nineteenth century. They are "conservatives" only in terms of the short history of their own country. They claim that the authentic American tradition went off the rails with the mass liberalism of the New Deal and should return to the individualism of the founding fathers. The makers of the Constitution took their philosophy from the first wave of modernity; the spirit of the New Deal belonged to the later waves of liberalism. In this sense, Goldwater is an American conservative. But what he conserves is the liberal philosophy of Locke. The founders of the United States took their thought from the eighteenth-century Enlightenment. Their rallying cry was "freedom." There was no place in their cry for the organic conservatism that pre-dated the age of progress. Indeed, the United States is the only society on earth that has no traditions from before the age of progress. Their "right-wing" and "left-wing" are just different species of liberalism. "Freedom" was the slogan of both Goldwater and President Johnson.[22]

The clobbering of Goldwater at the polls in November of 1964 shows how little the American people cared about the early liberalism of their founders. Johnson's "Great Society" expressed the new American "freedom" far better than Goldwater's talk of limited government and

22 In an earlier day, this was one respect in which Canada could be differentiated from the United States. Canadians had memories of a conservative tradition that was more than covert liberalism. At their best, Canadian conservatives never stood on an abstract appeal to free enterprise. They were willing to use the government to protect the common good. They were willing to restrain the individual's freedom in the interests of the community. The recent conservatism of Toronto, as expressed by the *Globe and Mail*, is American, not Canadian, conservatism. They call for the protection of property from government interference. Canadian Goldwaterism shows how much Toronto is now in spirit a part of the United States.

free enterprise. The majority tradition in the United-States backs Roosevelt, Kennedy, Johnson, whose liberalism is the most modern. The older liberalism of the Constitution had its swan song in the election of 1964. The classes that had once opposed Roosevelt were spent forces by 1964. The leaders of the new capitalism supported Johnson. Goldwater's cry for limited government seemed as antediluvian to the leaders of the corporations as Diefenbaker's nationalism seemed to the same elements in Canada. Johnson was supported not only by such obvious groups as Negroes and labour but also by the new managerial bourgeoisie of the suburbs. The farmers, who were supposed to be the last bastion of individualism, were not slow in voting for the continuance of subsidies. Four of Goldwater's five states were from the South. This was the last-ditch stand of a local culture. But it is doomed to disappear as much as an indigenous French Canada. The Goldwater camp was outraged by the sustained attacks of the television networks and newspaper chains. Were they not aware who had become the American establishment since 1932? Corporation capitalism and liberalism go together by the nature of things. The establishment knew how to defend itself when threatened by the outrageous challenge of outsiders from Arizona. The American election of 1964 is sufficient evidence that the United States is not a conservative society. It is a dynamic empire spearheading the age of progress.

The foregoing is platitudinous. But one consequence of the argument is not always made explicit: the impossibility of conservatism as a viable political ideology in our era. The practical men who call themselves conservatives must commit themselves to a science that leads to the conquest of nature. This science produces such a dynamic society that it is impossible to conserve anything for long. In such an environment, all institutions and standards are constantly changing. Conservatives who attempt to be practical face a dilemma. If they are not committed to a dynamic technology, they cannot hope to make any popular appeal. If they are so committed, they cannot hope to be conservatives. For example, the most brilliant conservative of our era has only been able to preserve what he loves (the power and culture of

France) by gaining support for nationalism from the most advanced technocrats. De Gaulle has had immediate success, but in the long run he will have helped to build a Europe in which the particularities of France cannot hope to exist. Other examples are legion. These days even the Papacy attempts to liberalize itself.

The impossibility of conservatism in our epoch is seen in the fact that those who adopt that title can be no more than the defenders of whatever structure of power is at any moment necessary to technological change. They provide the external force necessary if the society is to be kept together. They are not conservatives in the sense of being the custodians of something that is not subject to change. They are conservatives, generally, in the sense of advocating a sufficient amount of order so the demands of technology will not carry the society into chaos.[23] Because they are advocates of nothing more than this external order, they have come to be thought of as objects of opprobrium by the generous-hearted.

23 The next wave of American "conservatism" is not likely to base its appeal on such unsuccessful slogans as the Constitution and free enterprise. Its leader will not be a gentleman who truly cares about his country's past. It will concentrate directly on such questions as "order in the streets" which are likely to become crucial in the years ahead. The battle will be between democratic tyrants and the authoritarians of the right. If the past is a teacher to the present, it surely says that democratic Caesarism is likely to be successful. In the fight between Sulla and Marius, it was the descendants of the latter who established the Julian line of emperors.

Chapter Six

THE IMPOSSIBILITY OF CONSERVATISM in our era is the impossibility of Canada. As Canadians we attempted a ridiculous task in trying to build a conservative nation in the age of progress, on a continent we share with the most dynamic nation on earth. The current of modern history was against us.

A society only articulates itself as a nation through some common intention among its people. The constitutional arrangements of 1791, and the wider arrangements of the next century, were only possible because of a widespread determination not to become part of the great Republic. Among both the French and the British, this negative intention sprang from widely divergent traditions. What both peoples had in common was the fact they both recognized, that they could only be preserved outside the United States of America. The French were willing to co-operate with the English because they had no alternative but to go along with the endurable arrangements proposed by the ruling power. Both the French and the British had limited common ground in their sense of social order – belief that society required a high degree of law, and respect for a public conception of virtue. Both would grant the state much wider rights to control the individual than was recognized in the libertarian ideas of the American constitution. If their different conservatisms could have become a conscious bond, this nation might have preserved itself. An indigenous society might have continued to exist on the northern half of this continent.

To see why this intention failed in Canada, it is necessary to look more closely at the origins of both the French and the British traditions to see what has happened to them. To start with the British, it would be foolish to over-emphasize the niceties of theory among those who came to the St. John Valley or Upper Canada in the late eighteenth and early nineteenth centuries. It is difficult to put into words the conservatism of the English-speaking peoples in the Atlantic colonies or Upper Canada. The manifold waves of differing settlers must not be simplified into any common pattern. Much of English-speaking conservatism was simply a loyalty based on the flow of trade, and therefore destined to change when that flow changed. To repeat, Diefenbaker spoke with telling historical sense when he mentioned the Annexation Manifesto in his last speech to Parliament before the defeat of his government in 1963. He pointed out the similiarity between the views of the Montreal merchants in 1849 and the wealthy of Toronto and Montreal in 1963. In neither case did they care about Canada. No small country can depend for its existence on the loyalty of its capitalists. International interests may require the sacrifice of the lesser loyalty of patriotism. Only in dominant nations is the loyalty of capitalists ensured. In such situations, their interests are tied to the strength and vigour of their empire.

This does not imply that the nationalism in Englishspeaking Canada was simply a front for interest. Many of its elements were shaped by that strange phenomenon, British conservatism, which led the settlers to try to build on the northern half of this continent an independent society. British conservatism is difficult to describe because it is less a clear view of existence than an appeal to an ill-defined past. The writings of Edmund Burke are evidence of this. Yet many of the British officials, many Loyalists, and later many immigrants felt this conservatism very strongly. It was an inchoate desire to build, in these cold and forbidding regions, a society with a greater sense of order and restraint than freedom-loving republicanism would allow. It was no better defined than a kind of suspicion that we in Canada could be less lawless and have a greater sense of propriety than the United States. The inherited determination not to be Americans allowed these British people to come to a *modus vivendi* with the more defined desires of the French. English-speaking Canadians have been called a dull, stodgy, and indeed costive lot. In these dynamic days, such qualities are particularly unattractive to the chic.[24] Yet our stodginess has made us a society of greater simplicity, formality, and perhaps even innocence than the people to the south. Whatever differences there were between the Anglicans and the Presbyterians, and however differently their theologians might interpret the doctrine of original sin, both communities believed that the good life made strict demands on self-restraint. Nothing was more alien to them than the "emancipation of the passions" desired in American liberalism. An ethic of self-restraint naturally looks with suspicion on utopian movements, which proceed from an ethic of freedom. The early leaders of British North America identified lack of public and personal restraint with the democratic Republic. Their conservatism was essentially the social doctrine that public order and tradition, in contrast to freedom and experiment, were central to the good life. The British Crown was a symbol of a continuing loyalty to the state – less equivocal than was expected from republicans. In our early expansions, this conservative nationalism expressed itself in the use of public control in the political and economic spheres. Our opening of the West differed from that of the United States, in that the law of the central government was used more extensively, and less reliance was placed on the free settler. Until recently, Canadians have been much more willing than Americans to use governmental control over economic life to protect the public good against private freedom. To repeat, Ontario Hydro, the CNR, and the CBC were all established by Conservative governments. The early establishment of Ontario Hydro succeeded because of the efforts of an administrator, a politician, and a journalist, all of whom wrapped themselves in the Union Jack in their efforts to keep the development of electric power out of the hands of individual freedom.[25]

24 In his recent book *The Scotch* (New York and Toronto: Macmillan, 1964), Professor J. K. Galbraith has patronized his ancestors from western Ontario in this vein. A great human advance has been made from the Presbyterian farm to the sophistication of Harvard.

25 The three men were Sir Adam Beck, Sir Richard Whitney, and "Black Jack" Robinson.

English-speaking Canadians had never broken with their origins in Western Europe. Many of them had continuing connections with the British Isles, which in the nineteenth century still had ways of life from before the age of progress. That we never broke with Great Britain is often said to prove that we are not a nation but a colony. But the great politicians who believed in this connection – from Joseph Howe and Robert Baldwin to Sir John A. Macdonald and Sir Robert Borden, and indeed to John G. Diefenbaker himself – make a long list. They did not see it this way, but rather as a relation to the font of constitutional government in the British Crown. Many Canadians saw it as a means of preserving at every level of our life – religious, educational, political, social – certain forms of existence that distinguish us from the United States.

To repeat what has been said earlier about the tragedy of Green and Diefenbaker, the end of the Canadian experiment was involved in the collapse of Western Europe, particularly in the disappearance of the British political tradition. Since 1945, the collapse of British power and moral force has been evident to nearly all the world. Its present position is the end-process of that terrible fate that has overtaken Western civilization in the last century. When the British ruling class rushed headlong into the holocaust of 1914, they showed their total lack of political wisdom. As much as anybody, they had been corrupted by the modern mania. Whatever the courage of Churchill in 1940, it must be remembered that he was one of those in the Liberal Cabinet of 1914 who pushed their nation into the intemperance of the earlier disaster. The best British and Canadian youth had their guts torn out in the charnel house of the First World War. To write of the collapse of Western Europe is not my purpose here, but one small result was to destroy Great Britain as an alternative pull in Canadian life.

The history of conservatism in Great Britain has been one of growing emptiness and ambiguity. A political philosophy that is centred on virtue must be a shadowy voice in a technological civilization. When men are committed to technology, they are also committed to continual change in institutions and customs. Freedom must be the first political principle – the freedom to change any order that stands in the way of technological advance. Such a society cannot take seriously the conception of an eternal order by which human actions are measured and defined. For some individuals it remains a heavenly insurance policy. Without the conception of such an order, conservatism becomes nothing but the defence of property rights and chauvinism, attractively packaged as appeal to the past. Great Britain was the chief centre from which the progressive civilization spread around the world. Politically it became the leading imperial power of the West. As Plato saw with unflinching clarity, an imperialistic power cannot have a conservative society as its home base. From Hooker to Coleridge, the English conservatives had less and less influence in their own society. The thinkers who increasingly influenced their society were the liberals, with their clear advocacy of freedom and the knowledge that history was on their side. Practical conservatives continued to exert influence. But the classes and institutions to which they belonged have disappeared. The more honest have simply fought rearguard actions; the more ambitious have twisted conservatism into a façade for class and imperial interests. By the second half of the nineteenth century, appeals to such institutions as the monarchy and the church become little more than the praising of formal rituals, residual customs, and museums. Politicians from Disraeli to Macmillan have applied the term "conservative" to themselves; this was hardly more than a nationalist desire to take as much from the age of progress as they could. Indeed, they were less and less competent to do even this. Canada exported to Great Britain a series of extreme buccaneers who assumed the name "British conservative" during its degenerate era.

British conservatism was already largely a spent force at the beginning of the nineteenth century when English-speaking Canadians were making a nation. By the twentieth century, its adherents in Britain were helping to make their country an island outpost in the American conquest of Europe. Was British conservatism likely, then, to continue as a force to make English-speaking Canada independent? If not, what would? The Laurentian Shield and the Eskimos? British tradition has provided us with certain political and legal institutions, some of which are better than their American counterparts. Our parliamentary and judicial institutions may be preferable to the American system, but there is no deep division of principle. Certainly none of the differences between the two sets of institutions are sufficiently important to provide the basis for an alternative culture on the northern half of this continent.

For all the fruitfulness of the British tradition in nineteenth-century Canada, it did not provide any radically different approach to the questions of industrial civilization. Canadians in particular felt the blessings of technology in an environment so hard that to master it needed courage. But conservatism must languish as technology increases. It was not conceivable that industrial society would be organized along essentially different principles from those to the south. Try to imagine whether Toronto could be a quite dissimilar community from Buffalo or Chicago, or Vancouver from Seattle, and this is to answer the question. What other kind of industrial civilization is likely to appear anywhere on earth, let alone on the northern frontier of Manifest Destiny?

Because of the British tradition, socialist movements have been stronger in Canada than in the United States. But socialism has been a weakening force in Canadian life since 1945. To repeat a previous generalization: democratic socialism is not, as it believed itself to be, the high crest of the wave of the future, but rather a phenomenon from the nineteenth century. Since 1945, the forces that will shape our future in the West show themselves to be bureaucratic state capitalism. The only time when democratic socialism was strong in Canadian industrial society was in Ontario during the utopian days at the end of the Second World War. But the Frost and Robarts régimes have shown what a feeble and transitory phenomenon that was. In Ontario, some form of planned economy was the only conceivable alternative to Americanization. But to have anticipated a socialist Ontario was to hope rather than to predict. Certainly its leadership could not have come from the good-natured utopians who led our socialist parties.

They had no understanding of the dependence of socialism and nationalism in the Canadian setting. Their confused optimism is seen in the
fact that they have generally acted as if they were "left-wing" allies of
the Liberal party. Socialist leadership in Canada has been largely a
pleasant remnant of the British nineteenth century – the Protestant
tabernacle turned liberal. Such a doctrine was too flaccid to provide any
basis for independence.[26]

To turn to the more formidable tradition, the French Canadians are
determined to remain a nation. During the nineteenth century, they
accepted almost unanimously the leadership of their particular
Catholicism – a religion with an ancient doctrine of virtue. After 1789,
they maintained their connection with the roots of their civilization
through their church and its city, which more than any other in the
West held high a vision of the eternal. To Catholics who remain
Catholics, whatever their level of sophistication, virtue must be prior to
freedom. They will therefore build a society in which the right of the
common good restrains the freedom of the individual. Quebec was not
a society that would come to terms with the political philosophy of
Jefferson or the New England capitalists.

Nevertheless, indigenous cultures are dying everywhere in the
modern world. French-Canadian nationalism is a last-ditch stand. The
French on this continent will at least disappear from history with more
than the smirks and whimpers of their English-speaking compatriots –
with their flags flying and, indeed, with some guns blazing. The reality
of their culture, and their desire not to be swamped, cannot save them

26 A temporary advantage for the New Democratic Party is the fact
   that the powerful have used their heavy artillery on Diefenbaker. In
   the meantime they neglected the socialists. In the past, the establishment has been able to keep its hands on both the big parties, which
   could be substituted for each other when the voters wanted a
   change. When they have re-established their control in the
   Conservative party and removed Diefenbaker, this advantage will
   cease. The farmers are weakening as a force in Canadian life and will
   not have to be reckoned with in the same way in the future.

from the inexorable facts in the continental case. Solutions vary to the problem of how an autonomous culture can be maintained in Quebec. But all the answers face the same dilemma: Those who want to maintain separateness also want the advantages of the age of progress. These two ends are not compatible, for the pursuit of one negates the pursuit of the other. Nationalism can only be asserted successfully by an identification with technological advance; but technological advance entails the disappearance of those indigenous differences that give substance to nationalism. The solutions to this dilemma, which were attempted in the last few years, illustrate its nature.

One solution was the régime directed by Duplessis. No province in Canada gave more welcoming terms to American capital than the government of Duplessis. At the same time, in questions of education, provincial autonomy, etc., Duplessis followed policies that won support from the rural episcopate. It is all very well for a practising politician to base his régime on the combined support of St. James St. and the traditional Church. The people would depend on the corporations for their employment, while accepting the paternal hand of the cleric in the parish and in the school. Did the clerics think this was the best way for their people to learn to live with industrialism? Surely they recognized that such a régime could not last; it would produce new classes in society ultimately more hostile to Catholicism than to capitalism.

René Lévesque's solution to the problem, unlike Duplessis's liason with American capitalism, seems to attempt to build a semi-socialist society within the bounds of the province. The idea is to guarantee that the managerial élite be men of French culture, and that the control of the economy rest firmly in native hands. In such a scheme the continuance of Confederation is simply a question of convenience. If French civilization can be protected as a province within Confederation, then all well and good. If it cannot be, then separatism becomes a necessity. Lévesque's brilliant description of Laurier as "a black king" shows the seriousness of his intention.

There are two main difficulties in a semi-socialistic solution. The first of these is symbolized by the presence of Eric Kierans and George Marler as Ministers in the same government as Lévesque. The two men well represent the new and the old establishments of English-speaking Montreal. Provincial control of economic development is not only useful for French-Canadian nationalism but also for international capitalism. Any federal system of government strengthens the power of the corporations. The division of powers weakens the ability of public authority to control private governments; the size of the provinces allows them to be controlled by private economic power. The espousing by American or Canadian "conservatives" of greater authority for the local states has always a phoney ring about it, unless it is coupled with an appeal for the break-up of continental corporations. Decentralized government and continental corporations can lead in only one direction. In his criticism of Walter Gordon's budget in 1963, Kierans made a violent attack against any curbing of foreign investment as being a deterrent to economic growth.[27] As a Minister of the Quebec government, he accepts the thesis that economic growth is chiefly a responsibility of provincial governments. As regards provincial responsibility, Lévesque and Kierans are in agreement, but their motives for espousing responsibility are quite different. The motive of quick industrializing is surely likely to come in conflict with the motive of nationalism.

The financial pages of every newspaper are filled with announcements of French-speaking appointments to management. Continental capitalists have learnt that they are going to be in trouble if such appointments are not made. But when French nationalists derive satisfaction from these appointments, they would do well to remind themselves of the ancient adage: "I fear the Greeks, especially when they come with gifts." Corporations make concessions about management personnel for the sake of better relations with the alien community. These do not involve the basic control of the economy. Here the lines of

27 Kierans repeated this attack in a speech in Toronto in December of 1963.

battle will surely be drawn. How long will the people of Quebec be willing to pay the economic price of rejecting the terms laid down by big business for the development of power at Hamilton Falls? It is not likely that even such an unusual Liberal government as that of Prime Minister Lesage will be able to wrest control of the economy from the corporations and then keep it in the government's hands.[28]

The concession over French managerial personnel points to a greater chink in the nationalist armour. Lévesque presumably believes that the indigenous control of the French-Canadian economy will be maintained by the vote. Governments will retain final control of their economies through Socialistic measures by seeking electoral support. But is it to be expected that the new managerial élites will sustain their French culture for very long? If they work for continental corporations, will they not identify themselves with those corporations and vote for governments not interested in preserving national control of the economy? This is what happened in Ontario in the 1940's and 1950's. Even when much of the economy is socialized, the managers will gradually become indistinguishable from their international counterparts. To run a modern economy, men must be trained in the new technology over human and non-human nature. Such training cannot be reconciled with French-Canadian classical education. An élite trained in the modern way may speak French for many generations, but what other traditions will it uphold? The new social sciences are dissolvents of the family, of Catholicism, of classical education. It is surely more than a language that Lévesque wishes to preserve in his nation. New Orleans is a pleasant place for tourists. The dilemma remains. French Canadians must modernize their educational system if they are to have more than

28 The difference between the federal and provincial parties is wide, but not that wide. Indeed, Lévesque won a great victory when the provincial Liberals voted in their convention of 1964 that their party did not owe allegiance to the federal organization. Lévesque spent the federal election of 1963 in France. Presumably he could not stomach the policy of the federal Liberals on nuclear arms. His absence was a sop he had to pay for his membership in the party.

a peon's place in their own industrialization. Yet to modernize their
education is to renounce their particularity. At the heart of modern ⟵
liberal education lies the desire to homogenize the world. Today's
natural and social sciences were consciously produced as instruments
to this end.

In the immediate future, the wilder of the nationalist French-
Canadian youths may hope to build some kind of Castro-like state in
Quebec. As traditional Catholicism breaks up, there will be some excit-
ing moments. A Catholic society cannot be modernized as easily as a
Protestant one. When the dam breaks the flood will be furious.
Nevertheless, the young intellectuals of the upper-middle class will
gradually desert their existentialist nationalism and take the places
made for them in the continental corporations. The enormity of the
break from the past will arouse in the dispossessed youth intense forms
of beatness. But after all, the United States supports a large beat fringe.
Joan Baez and Pete Seeger titillate the *status quo* rather than threaten it.
Dissent is built into the fabric of the modern system. We bureaucratize
it as much as everything else. Is there any reason to believe that French
Canada will be different? A majority of the young is gradually patterned
for its place in the bureaucracies. Those who resist such shaping will
retreat into a fringe world of pseudo-revolt.

What does Lévesque think is the place of Catholicism in the continuing French fact? The young French Canadians who desire a better
society, because they grew up under Duplessis, believe in both nationalism and social freedom. Their liberalism is openly anti-Catholic and
even existentialist or Marxist. Others accept Catholicism but are determined that the Church should be disestablished. But the old Church
with its educational privileges has been the chief instrument by which
an indigenous French culture has survived in North America.
Liberalism is the ideological means whereby indigenous cultures are
homogenized. How then can nationalism and liberalism merge
together into a consistent political creed?

In 1918, Bourassa put the purposes of French-Canadian existence in
clear words:

Notre tâche à nous, Canadiens-français, c'est de prolonger en Amérique l'effort de la France chrétienne; c'est de défendre contre tout venant, le fallût-il contre la France elle-même, notre patrimoine religieux et national. Ce patrimoine, il n'est pas à nous seulement: il appartient à toute l'Amérique catholique, dont il est le foyer inspirateur et rayonnant; il appartient à toute l'Eglise, dont il est le principal point d'appui dans cette partie du monde; it appartient à toute la civilisation française, dont it est l'unique port de refuge et d'attache dans cette mer immense de l'américanisme saxonisant.[29]

Here is a national intention, beautifully expressed.

Bourassa's clarity about this intention was not matched by his understanding of what the twentieth century was going to be. He considered North America to be essentially *saxonisant* and dominated by an explicitly Protestant ethos – the "time is money" theology of a debased and secularized Calvinism. He lived in a world in which the British Empire still appeared a dominant force. Presumably he still thought of Latin America as in that twilight period of subservience to North America, which extended from the beginning of the nineteenth century.[30] Above all, Bourassa does not seem to have been aware of the effect of homogenization – what industrial civilization would do to all countries and all religions. Industrial culture had arisen in Protestant

29 See H. Bourassa, *La Langue, gardienne de la Foi* (Montreal, 1918). Freely translated: "Our special task as French Canadians, is to insert into America the spirit of Christian France. It is to defend against all comers, perhaps even against France herself, our religious and national heritage. This heritage does not belong to us alone. It belongs to all Catholic America. It is the inspiring and shining hearth of that America. It belongs to the whole Church, and it is the basic foundation of the Church in this part of the world. It belongs to ad French civilization of which it is the refuge and anchor amid the immense sea of saxonizing Americanism."

30 In Latin America there were 62 million in 1900, 120 million in 1950, 205 million in 1960. In the year 1955, North America ceased to have more people than South America.

societies and was the very form of *américanisme saxonisant* that
surrounded his nation. Bourassa seems therefore to have identified the
two, rather than to have recognized that technological culture was a
dissolvent of all national and religious traditions, not simply an expression of one of them. There is little of Gandhi's rejection of industrialism in his writings, but rather the positive assumption that the culture
of Quebec was French Christianity.[31] Nationalism was for him something essentially conservative – the maintenance in his part of the world
of the true way of life against the heresy of *américanisme saxonisant.*
This was a wasting and tragic dream for our dynamic era. Nevertheless,
despite his unawareness of the dynamism of the twentieth century, he
was surely right when he said that Catholicism as well as Frenchness
was necessary to make Quebec a nation.

Dynamic civilization has spread like oil over the surface of the world
during the half-century since Bourassa wrote. The twentieth century is
not something that belongs essentially to *l'américanisme saxonisant.* It
is no longer potential but actual in Quebec. Indeed, a wider question
arises here: What is the status of Catholicism in the age of progress?
Will a liberalized Catholicism accept industrialism and still be able to
shape it to a more human end? In Quebec, Catholicism will no longer
be *"Je me souviens,"* but a Catholicism appropriate to a vital present.
Lay education will not destroy the Church, but enable her to become
the spiritual leader of a free people. Accepting the age of progress, the
Church will give leadership to a more humane industrialism than has
arisen elsewhere in North America. It will provide the spiritual basis for
a continuing Franco-American civilization.

The possibility of such a Catholicism in Quebec cannot be discussed
apart from the relation of Catholicism to technology throughout the
world. That intricate question cannot be discussed at length in this
writing. Suffice it to say that, although the recent statements of the
Papacy seem optimistic about the Church's ability to live with our age,

31 France herself has always been a middle term between the dynamic
    civilization of Northern Europe and the more static culture of the
    Mediterranean.

it is still an open question whether Catholicism will be able to humanize mass Western society or be swept into the catacombs. What happens to the Catholic view of man, when Catholics are asked to shape society through the new sciences of biochemistry, physiological psychology, and sociology? These sciences arose from assumptions hostile to the Catholic view of man. Whatever the historical outcome, the ability of Catholicism to sustain a continuing Franco-American civilization appears dubious. If liberal Catholicism arises in Quebec, will it not be similar to the Catholicism of Cushing and Spellman, which is well-established within the assumptions of the American Empire?[32] Such a religion may have the same name, but it will be very different from the one Bourassa envisaged. The Church in America does not question the assumption of the society that permits it, except in the most general way. With this kind of Catholicism, industrialized Quebec would hardly be distinguishable from the rest of North America. Yet this is what the leading liberal clerics and laity seem to be establishing in the province. With such a moral heart, Quebec will soon blend into the continental whole and cease to be a nation except in its maintenance of residual patterns of language and personal habit.

Lévesque, at least, appears to be aware how difficult it will be to preserve the French fact on this continent. The French-Canadian liberals who plead for the continuance of Confederation and the extension of co-operative federalism seem to be more naïve. The confusion of these French-Canadian liberals is evident in a recent pronouncement by seven French-Canadian intellectuals under the title "An Appeal for Realism in Politics."[33] This pronouncement is considered by its authors to be a Canadian – not a French-Canadian – manifesto. It is an appeal

32 It is hard to imagine what Bourassa would have thought of the fact that it was a Catholic President of the United States of America (albeit a Teddy Roosevelt Catholic) who successfully applied pressure on the Canadian people for the acquisition of nudear arms.

33 This manifesto was published concurrently in French in *Cité Libre*, Montreal, and in English in *The Canadian Forum* (May, 1964), Toronto.

for the continuance of Confederation against the various parochialisms that threaten it. It puts forward the hope for a vital federalism that will accept the cultural diversity of Canada but will not be economically nationalist. It is not my purpose here to discuss its detailed proposals, but to quote its philosophical justification as an example of the present thought of French-Canadian liberal intellectuals. At the end of the manifesto, two reasons are given why the writers refuse to be "locked into a constitutional frame smaller than Canada." The second reason for this is described in the following language:

> *The most valid trends today are toward more enlightened human-ism, toward various forms of political, social, and economic univer-salism. Canada is a reproduction on a smaller and simpler scale of this universal phenomenon. The challenge is for a number of ethnic groups to learn to live together. It is a modern challenge, meaningful and indicative of what can be expected from man. If Canadians cannot make a success of a country such as theirs, how can they contribute in any way to the elaboration of humanism, to the formulation of the international structures of tomorrow? To confess one's inability to make Canadian Confederation work is, at this stage of history, to admit one's unworthiness to contribute to the universal order.*

Leaving aside such questions as what makes a trend "valid" and what are the conditions of human enlightenment, the point at issue is that the authors assert their faith in universalism and in the continued exis-tence of Canada at one and the same time. The faith in universalism makes it accurate to call the authors liberal. But how can a faith in universalism go with a desire for the continuance of Canada? The belief in Canada's continued existence has always appealed against universal-ism. It appealed to particularity against the wider loyalty to the conti-nent. If universalism is the most "valid modern trend," then is it not right for Canadians to welcome our integration into the empire? Canadian nationalism is a more universal faith than French-Canadian nationalism. But if one is a universalist, why should one stop at that point of particularity?

Many French-Canadian liberals seem to espouse "enlightened humanism" and universalism as against the parochial Catholicism that inhibited them personally and politically when it ruled their society. They seem to expect liberalism to purge Catholicism, but to maintain within itself all that was best in the ancient faith. In this manifesto, for example, the authors espouse the continuance of indigenous cultures and regret the victimizing of the "Indians, Métis, Orientals, Doukhobors, Hutterites, and dissidents of all kinds" in our past. They call for the democratic protection of such cultures. But do they not know that liberalism in its most unequivocal form (that is, untinged by memories of past traditions) includes not only the idea of universalism but also that of homogeneity? The high rhetoric of democracy was used when the Doukhobors were "victimized" under a French-Canadian Prime Minister. If the writers are to be truly liberal, they cannot escape the fact that the goal of their political philosophy is the universal and homogeneous state. If this is the noblest goal, then the idea of Canada was a temporary and misguided parochialism. Only those who reject that goal and claim that the universal state will be a tyranny, that is, a society destructive of human excellence, can assert consistently that parochial nationalisms are to be fought for. My purpose is not to debate at this point the question whether the "universal" values of liberalism lead to human excellence. What is indubitable is that those values go with internationalism rather than with nationalism. In this century, many men have known that the choice between internationalism and nationalism is the same choice as that between liberalism and conservatism. In a Canadian setting, internationalism means continentalism. French-Canadian liberalism does not seem to be the means whereby this nation could have been preserved.

All the preceding arguments point to the conclusion that Canada cannot survive as a sovereign nation. In the language of the new bureaucrats, our nation was not a viable entity. If one adds to this proposition the memory of the Liberals' policies, then one can truly say that the argument in their favour succeeds. They have been the best rulers for Canada because they have led the majority of us to accept necessity without much pain. *Fata volentem ducunt, nolentem trahunt.* Fate leads the willing, and drives the unwilling. The debt that we owe the Liberals is that they have been so willing to be led. The party has been made up of those who put only one condition on their willingness: that they should have personal charge of the government while our sovereignty disappears.

Canada has ceased to be a nation, but its formal political existence will not end quickly. Our social and economic blending into the empire will continue apace, but political union will probably be delayed. Some international catastrophe or great shift of power might speed up this process. Its slowness does not depend only on the fact that large numbers of Canadians do not want it, but also on sheer lethargy. Changes require decisions, and it is much easier for practising politicians to continue with traditional structures. The dominant forces in the Republic do not need to incorporate us. A branch-plant satellite, which has shown in the past that it will not insist on any difficulties in foreign or defence policy, is a pleasant arrangement for one's northern frontier. The pin-pricks of disagreement are a small price to pay. If the negotiations for union include Quebec, there will be strong elements in the United States that will dislike their admission. The kindest of all God's dispensations is that individuals cannot predict the future in detail. Nevertheless, the formal end of Canada may be prefaced by a period during which the government of the United States has to resist the strong desire of English-speaking Canadians to be annexed.

Chapter Seven

PERHAPS WE SHOULD REJOICE in the disappearance of Canada. We leave the narrow provincialism and our backwoods culture; we enter the excitement of the United States where all the great things are being done. Who would compare the science, the art, the politics, the entertainment of our petty world to the overflowing achievements of New York, Washington, Chicago, and San Francisco? Think of William Faulkner and then think of Morley Callaghan. Think of the Kennedys and the Rockefellers and then think of Pearson and E. P. Taylor. This is the profoundest argument for the Liberals. They governed so as to break down our parochialism and lead us into the future.

Before discussing this position, I must dissociate myself from a common philosophic assumption. I do not identify necessity and goodness. This identification is widely assumed during an age of progress. Those who worship "evolution" or "history" consider that what must come in the future will be "higher," "more developed," "better," "freer" than what has been in the past. This identification is also common among those who worship God according to Moses or the Gospels. They identify necessity and good within the rubric of providence. From the assumption that God's purposes are unfolded in historical events, one may be led to view history as an ever-fuller manifestation of good. Since the tenth century of the Christian era, some Western theologians have tended to interpret the fallen sparrow as if particular events could be apprehended by faith as good. This doctrine of providence was given its best philosophical expression by Hegel: *"Die Weltgeschichte ist das Weltgericht"* – "World history is the world's judgement." Here the doctrines of progress and providence have been brought together. But if history is the final court of appeal, force is the final argument. Is it possible to look at history and deny that within its dimensions force is the supreme ruler? To take a progressive view of providence is to come close to worshipping force. Does this not make us cavalier about evil? The screams of the tortured child can be justified by the achievements of history. How pleasant for the achievers, but how meaningless for the child.

As a believer, I must then reject these Western interpretations of providence. Belief is blasphemy if it rests on any easy identification of necessity and good. It is plain that there must be other interpretations of the doctrine. However massive the disaster we might face – for example, the disappearance of constitutional government for several centuries, or the disappearance of our species – belief in providence should be unaffected. It must be possible within the doctrine of providence to distinguish between the necessity of certain happenings and their goodness. A discussion of the goodness of Canada's disappearance must therefore be separated from a discussion of its necessity.

Many levels of argument have been used to say that it is good that Canada should disappear. In its simplest form, continentalism is the view of those who do not see what all the fuss is about. The purpose of life is consumption, and therefore the border is an anachronism. The forty-ninth parallel results in a lower standard of living for the majority to the north of it. Such continentalism has been an important force throughout Canadian history. Until recently it was limited by two factors. Emigration to the United States was not too difficult for Canadians, so that millions were able to seek their fuller future to the south. Moreover, those who believed in the primacy of private prosperity have generally been too concerned with individual pursuits to bother with political advocacy. Nevertheless, this spirit is bound to grow. One has only to live in the Niagara peninsula to understand it. In the mass era, most human beings are defined in terms of their capacity to consume. All other differences between them, like political traditions, begin to appear unreal and unprogressive. As consumption becomes primary, the border appears an anachronism, and a frustrating one at that.

The disadvantages in being a branch-plant satellite rather than in having full membership in the Republic will become obvious. As the facts of our society substantiate continentalism, more people will explicitly espouse it. A way of life shaped by continental institutions will produce political continentalism. Young and ambitious politicians will arise to give tongue to it. The election of 1963 was the first time in our history that a strongly nationalist campaign did not succeed, and that a government was brought down for standing up to the Americans. The ambitious young will not be slow to learn the lesson that Pearson so ably taught them about what pays politically. Some of the extreme actions of French Canadians in their efforts to preserve their society will drive other Canadians to identify themselves more closely with their southern neighbours than with the strange and alien people of Quebec.

Of course continentalism was more than a consumptionideology. In the nineteenth century, the United States appeared to be the haven of opportunity for those who had found no proper place in the older societies. Men could throw off the shackles of inequality and poverty in the new land of opportunity. To many Canadians, the Republic seemed a freer and more open world than the costive colonial society with its restraints of tradition and privilege. The United States appeared to be the best society the world had ever produced for the ordinary citizen. Whatever the mass society of prosperity has become, the idea that the United States is the society of freedom, equality, and opportunity will continue to stir many hearts. The affection and identification that a vast majority of Canadians have given to the publicly expressed ideals of such leaders as Roosevelt and Kennedy is evidence of this.

Continentalism as a philosophy is based on the liberal interpretation of history. Because much of our intellectual life has been oriented to Great Britain, it is not surprising that our chief continentalists have been particularly influenced by British liberalism. The writings of Goldwin Smith and F. H. Underhill carry more the note of Mill and Macaulay than of Jefferson and Jackson. This continentalism has made two main appeals. First, Canadians need the greater democracy of the Republic. To the continentalists, both the French and British traditions in Canada were less democratic than the social assumptions of the United States. In such arguments, democracy has not been interpreted solely in a political sense, but has been identified with social equality, contractual human relations, and the society open to all men, regardless of race or creed or class. American history is seen to be the development of the first mass democracy on earth.[34] The second appeal of continentalism is that humanity requires that nationalisms be overcome. In moving to larger units of government, we are moving in the direction of world order. If Canadians refuse this, they are standing back from the vital job of building a peaceful world. After the horrors that nationalistic wars have inflicted on this century, how can one have any sympathy for nationalism? Thank God the world is moving beyond such divisive loyalties.

Both these arguments were used with particular literacy by F. H. Underhill in his appeals for the Liberal party in the *Toronto Star* at the time of the 1963 election.[35] In his use of both these arguments it was sometimes difficult to know whether Underhill was appealing to the order of good or to the order of necessity, or whether in his mind the

34 In our generation this interpretation is expounded at length in the sermons of Arthur Schlesinger, Jr.

35 Professor F. H. Underhill is a key figure in the intellectual history of Canadian liberalism. See his book *In Search of Canadian Liberalism* (Toronto: Macmillan, 1960). Underhill gave many years to building the CCF. He found himself on the opposite side from the business community in Toronto on nearly every public question. Yet in a speech in Toronto in 1964, he could in his seventies announce that the liberal hope lies now with the great corporations. This conversion surely shows how consistently he continues to work out the consequences of his thought. He has recognized that the business community in America is no longer the propertied classes of his youth but managers whose ideology is liberal. He is right to believe that corporations and not doctrinaire socialism are the wave of the future.

two were identical. For example, closeness to the United States was identified in this writing with true internationalism. The argument from necessity is that nationalism must disappear and that we are moving inevitably to a world of continental empires. But this inevitable movement does not in itself mean that we are moving to a better and more peaceful world order. The era of continental rivalries may be more ferocious than the era of nationalisms. Only when one adds to this argument the liberal faith in progress does one believe that continentalism must be a step toward a nobler internationalism. The argument for continentalism is different when it appeals to inevitability than when it is based on the brotherhood of man. This ambiguity in Underhill was mirrored in the whole Liberal campaign of 1963, in which Pearson wrapped his acceptance of continental atomic arms in the language of international obligations and his loyalty to the United Nations.

To those outside the progressive view of history, there was a note of high comedy in the use of the Tennysonian "parliament of man" language to attack Diefenbaker's defence of national sovereignty, when the issue at stake was the acquisition of nuclear arms. The Sifton and Southam papers made any fear of dominance by the American Empire seem a retreat from true internationalism. This note of comedy went further in the summer of 1963, when the CBC made misty-eyed television programs about Pearson's return to the United Nations as the true Canadian internationalist, at a time when he was negotiating with the United States for the spread of nuclear arms to Canada.

However, laughter should not allow us to fail in charity toward liberalism. It was easier to use its language consistently in the era of Goldwin Smith than in the twentieth century. Liberalism was, in origin, criticism of the old established order. Today it is the voice of the establishment. It could sound a purer note when it was the voice of the outsider than today when it is required to legislate freedom. For example, Harvard liberalism was surely nobler when William James opposed the Spanish-American war than when Arthur Schlesinger, Jr., advised Kennedy on Cuban policy.

It has already been argued that, because of our modern assumptions about human good, Canada's disappearance is necessary.[36] In deciding whether continentalism is good, one is making a judgement about progressive political philosophy and its interpretation of history. Those who dislike continentalism are in some sense rejecting that progressive interpretation. It can only be with an enormous sense of hesitation that one dares to question modern political philosophy. If its assumptions are false, the age of progress has been a tragic aberration in the history of the species. To assert such a proposition lightly would be the height of irresponsibility. Has it not been in the age of progress that disease and overwork, hunger and poverty, have been drastically reduced? Those who criticize our age must at the same time contemplate pain, infant mortality, crop failures in isolated areas, and the sixteen-hour day. As soon as that is said, facts about our age must also be remembered: the increasing outbreaks of impersonal ferocity, the banality of existence in technological societies, the pursuit of expansion as an end in itself. Will it be good for men to control their genes? The possibility of nuclear destruction and mass starvation may be no more terrible than that of man tampering with the roots of his humanity. Interference with human nature seems to the moderns the hope of a higher species in the ascent of life; to others it may seem that man in his pride could corrupt his very being. The powers of manipulation now available may portend the most complete tyranny imaginable. At least, it is feasible to wonder whether modern assumptions may be basically inhuman.

To many modern men, the assumptions of this age appear inevitable, as being the expression of the highest wisdom that the race has distilled. The assumptions appear so inevitable that to entertain the

36 In our day, necessity is often identified with some fad in the atoms or the "life force." But historical necessity is chiefly concerned with what the most influential souls have thought about human good. Political philosophy is not some pleasant cultural game reserved for those too impotent for practice. It is concerned with judgements about goodness. As these judgements are apprehended and acted upon by practical men, they become the unfolding of fate.

possibility of their falsity may seem the work of a madman. Yet these assumptions were made by particular men in particular settings. Machiavelli and Hobbes, Spinoza and Vico, Rousseau and Hegel, Marx and Darwin, originated this account of human nature and destiny. Their view of social excellence was reached in conscious opposition to that of the ancient philosophers. The modern account of human nature and destiny was developed from a profound criticism of what Plato and Aristotle had written. The modern thinkers believed that they had overcome the inadequacies of ancient thought, while maintaining what was true in the ancients.

Yet Plato and Aristotle would not have admitted that their teachings could be used in this way. They believed that their own teaching was the complete teaching for all men everywhere, or else they were not philosophers. They believed that they had considered all the possibilities open to man and had reached the true doctrine concerning human excellence. Only the thinkers of the age of progress considered the classical writers as a preparation for the perfected thought of their own age. The classical philosophers did not so consider themselves. To see the classics as a preparation for later thought is then to think within the assumptions of the age of progress. But this is to beg the question, when the issue at stake is whether these assumptions are true. It is this very issue that is raised by the tragedies and ambiguities of our day.[37]

Ancient philosophy gives alternative answers to modern man concerning the questions of human nature and destiny. It touches all the central questions that man has asked about himself and the world. The classical philosophers asserted that a universal and homogeneous state would be a tyranny. To elucidate their argument would require an account of their total teaching concerning human beings. It would take

37 The previous paragraph is dependent on the writings of Professor Leo Strauss who teaches at the University of Chicago. For Strauss's account of political philosophy, see, for example, *What Is Political Philosophy* (Glencoe: The Free Press, 1959) and *The City and Man* (Chicago: Rand McNally, 1964). I only hope that nothing in the foregoing misinterprets the teaching of that wise man.

one beyond political philosophy into the metaphysical assertion that changes in the world take place within an eternal order that is not affected by them. This implies a definition of human freedom quite different from the modern view that freedom is man's essence. It implies a science different from that which aims at the conquest of nature.

The discussion of issues such as these is impossible in a short writing about Canada. Also, the discussion would be inconclusive, because I do not know the truth about these ultimate matters. Therefore, the question as to whether it is good that Canada should disappear must be left unsettled. If the best social order is the universal and homogeneous state, then the disappearance of Canada can be understood as a step toward that order. If the universal and homogeneous state would be a tyranny, then the disappearance of even this indigenous culture can be seen as the removal of a minor barrier on the road to that tyranny. As the central issue is left undecided, the propriety of lamenting must also be left unsettled.

My lament is not based on philosophy but on tradition. If one cannot be sure about the answer to the most important questions, then tradition is the best basis for the practical life. Those who loved the older traditions of Canada may be allowed to lament what has been lost, even though they do not know whether or not that loss will lead to some greater political good. But lamentation falls easily into the vice of self-pity. To live with courage is a virtue, whatever one may think of the dominant assumptions of one's age. Multitudes of human beings through the course of history have had to live when their only political allegiance was irretrievably lost. What was lost was often something far nobler than what Canadians have lost. Beyond courage, it is also possible to live in the ancient faith, which asserts that changes in the world, even if they be recognized more as a loss than a gain, take place within an eternal order that is not affected by their taking place. Whatever the difficulty of philosophy, the religious man has been told that process is not all. *"Tendebantque manus ripae ulterioris amore."*[38]

38 Virgil, *Aeneid* (Book VI): "They were holding their arms outstretched in love toward the further shore."

About the Author

George P. Grant (1918–1988) was educated at Queen's University and Oxford. He taught philosophy and later political science at Dalhousie University, and chaired the Department of Religion at McMaster. One of the foremost Canadian political thinkers of our time, he was the author of *Philosophy in the Mass Age* (1959), *Technology and Empire* (1969), *English-Speaking Justice* (1974), and *Technology and Justice* (1986) as well as the seminal *Lament for a Nation* (1965).